Welcome Aboard!

Bon Voyage! The cruise ship *Cunard Princess* is ready to sail.

Welcome Aboard!

Traveling on an Ocean Liner

Barbara A. Huff

Foreword by John Maxtone-Graham

illustrated with photographs

Clarion Books

TICKNOR & FIELDS: A HOUGHTON MIFFLIN COMPANY

New York

For my mother

Photo credits: Unless otherwise credited, all photos are by
the author. Special thanks to Barry M. Winiker in New York
for the use of eight photos from the Cruise Ship Project.

Clarion Books
Ticknor & Fields, a Houghton Mifflin Company
Copyright © 1987 by Barbara A. Huff

Library of Congress Cataloging-in-Publication Data
Huff, Barbara A.
Welcome aboard!

Bibliography: p.
Includes index.
Summary: Describes, in text and illustrations, a
five-day Atlantic crossing aboard the QE2. Also
discusses the history of steamships and includes
information about island cruises and places where
one may go to see large ships.
1. Queen Elizabeth 2 (Ship)—Juvenile literature.
2. Ocean liners—Juvenile literature. 3. Historic
ships—Juvenile literature. [1. Queen Elizabeth 2 (Ship)
2. Ocean liners] I. Title.
VM383.Q32H84 1987 387.2 432 86-34315
ISBN 0-89919-503-2
A 10 9 8 7 6 5 4 3 2 1

Acknowledgments

Many people helped me with *Welcome Aboard!* My special thanks go to John Maxtone-Graham, who generously offered to read the manuscript and made numerous helpful suggestions. If any errors remain, they are mine. I also want to thank him for writing such a splendid foreword.

A deep bow goes to my editor, Ann Troy, who saw me through this maiden voyage with skill, ingenuity, and grace.

At the Cunard office in New York, Susan Alpert has been an enormous help with pictures and information, and Nancy Brookes, as always, with reservations and useful advice. My thanks also to Ralph Bahna, president and managing director of Cunard, for his encouragement.

Aboard the *QE2*, Captain Lawrence Portet and his sterling crew deserve my heartiest appreciation. And last on the list but first in my affections, thanks to all my friends in the crew; they make every voyage a homecoming.

Contents

Foreword

Some years ago, I crossed westbound on *QE2* with a very old friend and his wife from London who had never been ocean liner passengers before. We all boarded with keenest anticipation and booked a table in the Queen's Grill. After coffee that first night, following an excellent dinner, my friend reached for his wallet and inquired how we should divide up the bill. I was delighted to inform him that the price of his passage had included all of his meals.

Of course, if he had read Barbara Huff's admirable book as either a child or an adult, he would have known this already, plus a very great deal more about life on board an ocean liner. Ms. Huff has seen fit to include a wealth of on-board routine, not only day-to-day information and how-tos of all kinds, but also an enrichment of maritime history and shipboard lore that taught me several things I had not known before.

For new young passengers—and their parents—either crossing the Atlantic or cruising anywhere in the world, I cannot recommend too highly this compendium of facts, suggestions, tips, and trivia. I remember from my own childhood as well as crossings with my children that an ocean liner is a paradise for the young of all ages, full of adventure, new sights and sounds and a host of friends, whether fellow passengers or staff and crew.

Shipboard, after a near brush with disaster, is back with us, and nothing could be more timely or appropriate than attracting and educating tomorrow's passengers with this excellent book. Bravo, Barbara Huff, and bon voyage to all who are wise enough to read it before they sail!

John Maxtone-Graham

Introduction

There is nothing—absolutely nothing—half so much worth doing as simply messing about in boats.

KENNETH GRAHAME, *The Wind in the Willows*

The exciting and glamorous story of ocean liners almost ended twenty years ago. The villains that threatened those large passenger ships with extinction were jet planes and high fuel costs. But like many other endangered species, the ocean liner is back, and healthier than ever.

The new popularity of liners happened suddenly, in the late 1970s and early 1980s. Plane fares went up and travelers were lured to liners by good prices, new ships, and a much wider choice of places to visit. Ship travel is thriving, and surveys show more families than ever before are enjoying shipboard life.

Since 1840 steamships called ocean liners have carried paying passengers across the Atlantic between the United States

Ocean Pictures (Cruising) Ltd Southampton, England

The *QE2* manuevers through the Panama Canal to the Pacific Ocean on her way around the world.

and Europe. Shipping companies such as the Cunard Line operated lines of ships that crossed the ocean on a regular schedule, like ferryboats. For a long time, there were so many ships that they were called the Atlantic Ferry. The ships that formed that "line" across the ocean became known as liners.

Today only Cunard's *Queen Elizabeth 2*, usually called the *QE2*, makes frequent transatlantic crossings, although many other liners cross now and then.

Passenger ships may not cross the Atlantic the way they once did, but ship travelers can now explore all the world's oceans, and many rivers as well, on cruises.

Cruise is a more familiar word than *crossing* these days. There's a difference. A cruise is a round-trip. Sometimes the cruise ship takes you to a port—Bermuda, for instance—and stays there for a few days. You go ashore during the day and go back to the ship at night. Then the ship returns you to where you started.

A cruise may take you to one or two ports, or to dozens. Several ships make cruises around the world. You can even sail out to sea on an ocean liner and go nowhere at all. Cruises to nowhere are very popular, and a good way to get a taste of liner travel.

On a crossing you go from one place to another and get off. Cunard will sell you a ticket to Southampton, England. Most passengers get off there and go back by ship or plane some time later.

You can, however, "turn around with the ship" in Southampton and go back to the States, usually getting both crossings for the price of one. Even if you turn around with the ship, you will have to get off and spend the night on shore. You can't stay on board, as you do on a cruise.

This book shows you what it's like to make a crossing on the *QE2*. Activities vary from ship to ship, but the nonstop entertainment offered on the *QE2* is typical of the fun on ships, whether crossing or cruising.

It was the Cunard Line that first said, "Getting there is half the fun." I think you'll see why.

Have a good crossing!

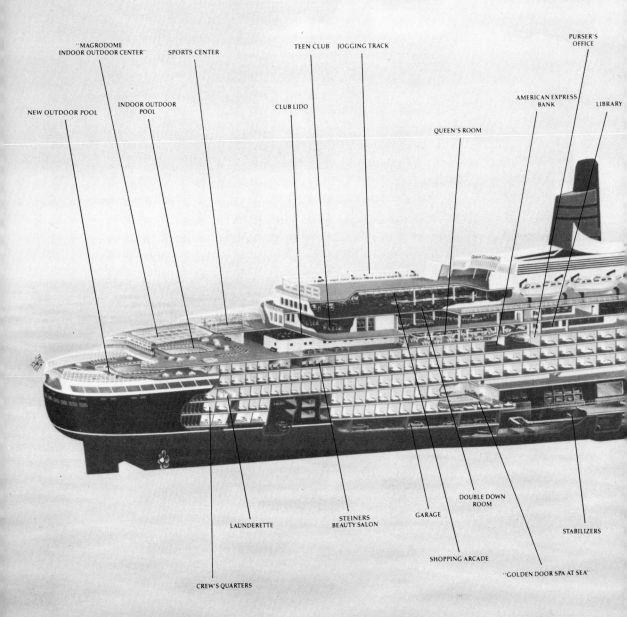

"MAGRODOME
INDOOR OUTDOOR CENTER"

SPORTS CENTER

TEEN CLUB   JOGGING TRACK

PURSER'S
OFFICE

NEW OUTDOOR POOL

INDOOR OUTDOOR
POOL

CLUB LIDO

AMERICAN EXPRESS
BANK

LIBRARY

QUEEN'S ROOM

LAUNDERETTE

STEINERS
BEAUTY SALON

GARAGE

DOUBLE DOWN
ROOM

STABILIZERS

CREW'S QUARTERS

SHOPPING ARCADE

"GOLDEN DOOR SPA AT SEA"

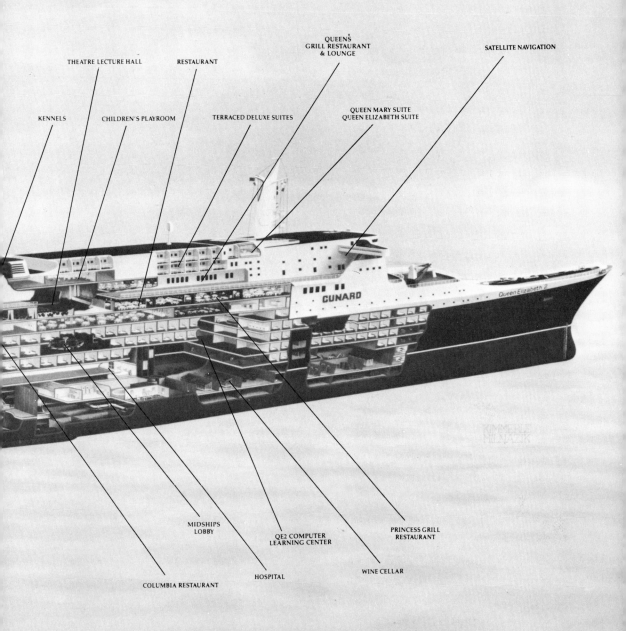

QUEEN'S GRILL RESTAURANT & LOUNGE

SATELLITE NAVIGATION

THEATRE LECTURE HALL

RESTAURANT

KENNELS

CHILDREN'S PLAYROOM

TERRACED DELUXE SUITES

QUEEN MARY SUITE
QUEEN ELIZABETH SUITE

CUNARD

Queen Elizabeth 2

MIDSHIPS LOBBY

QE2 COMPUTER LEARNING CENTER

PRINCESS GRILL RESTAURANT

HOSPITAL

WINE CELLAR

COLUMBIA RESTAURANT

1

Sailing Day

Now, voyager, sail thou forth to seek and find.

WALT WHITMAN

To travel hopefully is a better thing than to arrive.

ROBERT LOUIS STEVENSON

"All persons not sailing with the ship are requested to disembark immediately, as the *QE2* will be leaving in a few minutes. All persons not sailing with the ship . . ."

It is almost 4:30 on a hot summer afternoon in New York harbor, and the *QE2* is preparing to sail. The three-thousand-mile crossing from New York to Southampton, on the southern coast of England, will take five days.

You are among the hundreds of passengers who crowd the ship's railings. Some, like you, look down on the dock fifty feet below. Other passengers look across the pier to an elevated parking area where friends and relatives have gathered to watch the sailing.

At the ship's bow and stern, tugboats nose into position. They will guide the ship out of the dock and through the busy harbor.

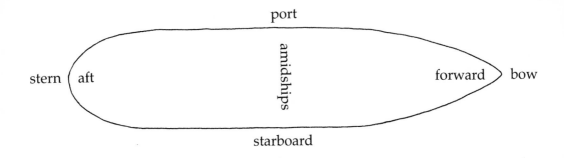

port

amidships

stern (aft

forward) bow

starboard

It's easy to remember that port means left — both have four letters.

One of the ship's crew passes out packages of colored streamers called serpentines. Each package has several rolls of colored paper, wound like videotape and easy to throw a long way.

You have noticed that the *QE2* is still attached to the dock by heavy ropes called hawsers and by several gangways bridging the gap between ship and pier. One or two of the gangways are for passengers and look like those tunnels you walk through to get on an airplane. Near the bow are ramps the crew use to enter the ship. Other gangways far below are for loading baggage and supplies.

Near the stern, just above the water level, there is a ramp for loading cars. Cars drive right off the dock onto the ramp and into an opening in the ship's side. From there they go into an elevator that takes them down a few decks to the garage area.

As you begin throwing streamers over the railing, your heart beats a little faster. You sense an excitement flowing along through the passengers near you.

Let's suppose that you are a young person traveling with your parents and sister, who is preschool age. Your parents have gone to the children's playroom to sign up your sister for the little kids' activities, and will be along later. But you don't want to miss a thing, so that's why you are at the rail, surrounded by friendly strangers.

A boy standing next to you points toward the parking lot, where a group of people is tossing streamers across to the ship. You each manage to catch a streamer and you tie them side by side to the rail. You've met your first shipboard friend.

All around you people laugh and chatter and take pictures of each other, of the tugs and the city skyline, of the colored streamers. Soon a web of blue and red and yellow and green streamers ties the ship to the people on the shore.

Now when you look down at the dock, longshoremen are moving the gangways aside. No one else can come aboard; no one can leave. A murmur of anticipation goes through the passengers around you as they watch the dockworkers let loose the lines that have been looped around bollards — thick wooden or metal posts — on the dock.

The ship's whistle, not far above your head, gives a mighty blast. For a second, just a second, the chatter and laughter and calling back and forth from ship to shore die to a whisper.

You realize the ship is moving. The strip of water between ship and dock is wider. The web of streamers stretches tight. Here a green thread snaps, there the blue and yellow threads tear and fall back against the pier and down into the water.

The whistle sounds again, followed by a last agitated waving and calling from the passengers. Now the colored strands have all broken. There is no more tie to the shore. It is a thrilling moment, and a moving one.

If your eyes feel a bit teary and your throat a little tight, you're not the only one. I've sailed on big ships dozens of times and I've always felt that excitement, always been moved at that first moment of being freed from the land.

There is an element of relief in those first moments, too. A lot of planning, not to mention daydreaming, has preceded your sailing day.

Most people plan vacation trips for months. I think it's a good idea for a whole family to plan trips together. Once you've decided to travel by ship, information is available from many places. Ads in newspapers often have phone numbers to call or coupons to send in. Travel agents and shipping companies are glad to supply information.

A typical shipping line brochure has photographs of various kinds of cabins and of the public rooms, pools, and activities. There's always a list of sailing dates and prices. Ships usually offer special prices for children.

Ship brochures include deck plans — a series of little maps showing where everything is. The QE2 is thirteen stories high and as long as three football fields. Cunard calls her a city at sea. Spending a little time with the deck plan before your trip will help you find your way around once on board.

Bedrooms on ships are called cabins, or sometimes staterooms. Some cabins have bunk beds, some regular beds. All cabins on the QE2, and on most ships, have bathrooms, radios, and telephones, and are air-conditioned.

Parents traveling with a young child usually ask for an extra bed in their cabin so the child can sleep with them. Older children can have cabins of their own.

Perhaps, after hours spent poring over piles of brochures, deck plans, maps, and travel guides, you had a family conference. The decision was to sail to England on the QE2, travel in Europe for two weeks, and fly back home.

Cunard, like most lines, includes airfare in the ticket price. Often a telephone call to a travel agent or shipping line is all it takes to arrange everything.

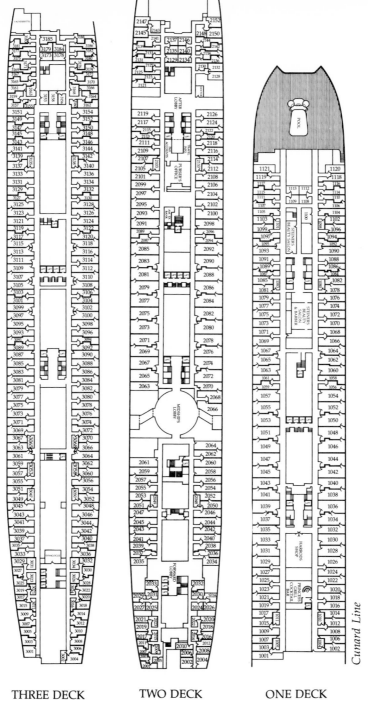

THREE DECK TWO DECK ONE DECK

Cunard Line

Passengers use deck plans for choosing cabins and getting to know the ship.

Your tickets came in the mail in a fat envelope. With them were tags to put on your luggage, instructions about getting to the dock, and information about sailing times and necessary documents.

For this trip all you needed besides the tickets was a passport for each of you. Children used to be included on their parents' passports, but now even the youngest baby needs one.

People apply for passports at passport agencies, federal and state courts, and at some post offices. Everyone over thirteen must apply in person when getting a passport for the first time. Your travel agent, or a steamship or airline representative can tell you where to apply in your part of the country.

A U.S. passport is a small, twenty-four-page book with a dark-blue cover on which the seal of the United States is printed in gold. Inside are your photograph and places for your name, address, and other information.

You and your family arrived at the passenger ship terminal on the Hudson River in New York City two hours before the 4:45 P.M. sailing time.

Porters took your suitcases, and a long escalator carried you up to the dock. You waited in line a few minutes, went through a security check, and showed your tickets and passports to a Cunard employee. Out of sight somewhere, your luggage was having a security check, too.

Just before going aboard, your photos were taken. Tomorrow, all the sailing day photos — five-by-seven color prints — will be on display, and you can buy as many as you like, or none at all. The ship's photographers take pictures throughout the voyage. I have drawers full.

Then you walked up a gangway and stepped through an opening in the ship's side into an area called the Midships

Lobby. A member of the crew greeted you with a cheerful "Welcome aboard!" Then he or she asked your cabin numbers and showed you where the cabins were.

Your cabins are on Two Deck, not far from the passenger gangway. I think I'll put you in 2034, one of my favorite cabins on the QE2, and the rest of the family next door in 2036.

You know from the deck plan that Two Deck is in the middle of the ship, with six decks and the engine room below and six decks above. Both 2034 and 2036 are outside cabins. That means they have portholes, the ship word for windows. The deck plan also shows that the passenger decks below and above you have both outside and inside cabins. The inside cabins, without portholes, are smaller and less expensive.

These days, all ships are air-conditioned and have stabilizers — fins that come out from the ship's side underwater and keep the ship from rolling too badly in a heavy sea. The steadiest part of a ship is the center — amidships — on a middle deck. But except in a storm, even cabins near the bow and stern, or up high, have little movement.

You didn't spend much time in the cabin when you first came aboard an hour ago. A quick look showed a bed and chair, lots of drawer and closet space, a bathroom stocked with shampoo, soap, a shower cap, and other little presents. There are flowers from Cunard. Your parents' cabin next door has the same things, but it's bigger and there's a third bed for your sister.

On the floor near the door were some forms to fill out — you gave them to your parents — and a day's program. The program for sailing day always has a picture of the captain and a welcoming message from him. Inside it, you read that dinner is from 7:30–9:00, that there is a first-run movie in the theater at 10:00, live entertainment, music, and dancing in several

Tugs are small, but powerful. Large ships can maneuver in and out of a harbor without them, but it isn't easy.

places, and a get-together of teens and preteens at 9:30.

Also under the door was a bulletin with announcements of the entertainers on board and upcoming events, and pictures of the cruise staff, who organize all entertainment during the crossing.

Now you are up on deck, not wanting to miss a minute of the sailing. As tugs nudge the ship away from the dock and she turns her bow downriver, you join hundreds of passengers crowding the forward observation area high up near the front of the ship.

Look to port. The New York skyline seems even more dramatic than in all the pictures you've seen. As the ship nears the southern end of Manhattan Island, everyone turns to starboard to watch the beautiful, refurbished Statue of Liberty, setting sun behind her, holding up her lamp "beside the golden door."

The unforgettable New York skyline.

Once through the harbor, the *QE2* sails under the Verrazano Narrows Bridge, and you are in the Atlantic. Three thousand miles of open ocean lie in front of you. Perhaps the ship isn't so big after all.

Now that the sailing is over, it's hard for you to decide what to do next. You wander around the ship a bit. You find orchestras playing in the two big lounges — in the Queen's Room and in the Grand Lounge, usually called the Double Room, because it is just that, a double room. The lower level, called the Double Down, has the dance floor and a big area filled with tables and chairs. You finally decide to go back to your cabin and unpack your suitcases. By the time everyone in your family is settled in, it's time for dinner.

Tonight you all eat together in the Columbia Restaurant. The *QE2* has four dining rooms. The price of your cabin determines where you eat. Tomorrow, if your sister doesn't want to wait until 7:30 for dinner, she can join other young children at 6:00 in a special section of the Columbia. She'll find a children's menu and friends from the children's playroom for company.

Anyone over seven or eight years old eats at the family's table. Even very experienced restaurant-goers often need help from the friendly waiters to get them through an ocean liner's menu.

After dinner you go to the teen club for a brief meeting with the teen counselors. They tell you about the activities planned for the crossing and give you programs for the preteen and teen events. The room is full of young people ranging from seven or eight years to high school age.

The preteen program includes a video game competition, dodgeball, swimming, a scavenger hunt, computer Olympics, a Ping-Pong tournament, a costume party, and a farewell disco night.

The teen program also has computer Olympics and the costume party, Ping-Pong, and swimming. In addition, it includes water volleyball, Trivial Pursuit, shuffleboard, an autograph hunt, and a farewell party in the Club Lido. Everyone is invited to a movie every night.

By 10:00 a lot is going on around the ship — music, dancing, a movie, gambling in the casino. But if you go out on deck you will find yourself alone. Few people seem to understand that you can dance and see movies and hear music at home, but you can be part of night at sea only on the open deck of a ship.

I always go out last thing at night. The best place to stand is on the stern, as far back as you can go. It's not too windy there, and you can watch the wake, that white foaming line of water streaming out behind the ship.

It's usually misty on the North Atlantic, but maybe once

during a crossing the sky is clear, the stars sparkle, and there may even be a moon. I can't think of anything more gorgeous than a moonlit night on the ocean.

Sea air is apt to be cool — put on a coat before going out. It will probably be a little wet underfoot from the sea spray. My dress-up shoes have a permanent saltwater line around the soles from my walks on deck at night. The salt line on my shoes always reminds me of night at sea aboard ship.

After you've been out on deck for a while, lick a fingertip. It will taste salty from the sea mist in the air. You'll sleep well tonight, the first night of your crossing.

2

Day Two

It would take one person four months to partic-
ipate in all the activities offered on board the
QE2 on one five-day crossing.

THE *QE2 Times*

"Ladies and gentlemen, may I have your attention, please.
You should now be standing at your emergency sta-
tions. . . ."

Not to worry, it's just lifeboat drill. At 10:30 in the morning
of the first full day at sea, all passengers are urged to attend
the lifeboat drill. It's important to know where in the cabin
your life jacket is kept, how to put it on, and what to do next.

The lifeboat station for cabin 2034 is near the roulette wheel
in the casino, without a lifeboat in sight. As an officer explains
in a recorded message, you might in an emergency have to
wait for some time, and it's better to be inside.

If it became necessary, the lifeboats carried high up on the
ship would be lowered to where you are waiting, and you
would embark through doors in the ship's side. The crew has
lifeboat drill, too. You may try to get a book out of the library

one day and find a sign on the door: "Gone to lifeboat drill. Back in half an hour." Passengers stand comfortably inside during drills. Crew members take turns actually getting into the boats and being lowered to the water.

Long before lifeboat drill, any sensible first-time passenger will have a huge breakfast and go explore the ship. Let's start at the bottom. You'll soon see why Cunard calls the QE2 a city at sea. Even smaller liners have many similar facilities.

The lowest deck a passenger can visit on the QE2 is Seven Deck. One of the swimming pools is down there, as well as a gym and massage rooms. On Six Deck are another pool, hot tubs, and more exercise equipment. Organized activities include water exercises, aerobics classes, and an all-out fitness program. Some people spend a whole crossing putting on weight in the dining room and taking it off in the health club.

The crew has lifeboat drill, just as the passengers do. Crew members actually get into the boats and are lowered to the water.

The rest of Six and Seven Decks and the area below them are off limits to passengers. That's where the wine cellar, the hospital, the stabilizers, the engine room, some of the crew quarters, and the garage are located. Your family can bring a car on board. If you have forty cars, you can bring them all. That's how much space there is.

We'll skip most of Five, Four, and Three Decks. Those decks are mostly cabins — passengers in the center, crew near the bow and stern. Three Deck has a launderette and a synagogue.

Two Deck is your home deck and it also has the cashier and travel desk, the doctor's office, and the Bureau. The Bureau is the ship's office, with a staff who can answer questions about almost anything. Across from the Bureau is the bank, where tellers cash travelers checks and change your dollars into foreign money.

One Deck contains mostly cabins, plus the hairdresser and the chiropodist — the foot doctor. Her office is in a little side passage off the main alleyway. Ship people use the word *alleyway* instead of corridor or hall.

Astern on One Deck is a multitiered outdoor pool and a place to sit. At lunchtime, hot dogs and hamburgers are available there for passengers who want to stay out on the deck all day. Since cruises go to warm-weather places, a lot more outdoor eating goes on than during crossings. On the North Atlantic, the weather is changeable, to put it mildly.

The next deck up is called Quarter Deck on the *QE2*. There is no rule about naming decks. The *Bohème* sailing out of Saint Petersburg, Florida, has a Bahama Deck and an Antilles Deck. *Homeric*, cruising between Bermuda and New York, has a Pacific Deck. *World Discoverer*, traveling to Antarctica, has a Spa Deck and an Odyssey Deck.

QE2's Quarter Deck has the Columbia, the main first-class dining room, and the small, elegant Princess Grill, for people in more expensive first-class cabins.

The main kitchens are forward of the dining rooms. Passengers can arrange a kitchen tour by asking the Columbia's manager. If you go through the kitchens, wear sneakers. It's very slippery in there. Oh, and no samples.

Just as a hotel is always changing things around, redecorating, repainting, a ship makes frequent changes, too. A few years ago a contraption called the Magrodome was installed on Quarter Deck over the pool and disco. The Magrodome is a glass roof that slides open to let in the sun and then slides shut again to keep out everything else.

On the North Atlantic, the Magrodome is usually closed up tight. On cruises and the rare sunny days on crossings, the Magrodome slides open, with much clanking of machinery, and the whole pool area is open to the sky.

In the middle of the Quarter Deck is a well-stocked library. In 1982, the *QE2* became the first ship to have full-time, professionally trained librarians in charge of the ship's library. Before that a crew member sat at a desk and checked books in and out.

The Quarter Deck library has four thousand volumes and subscribes to dozens of magazines. The catalogue is computerized, a help when the ship is full and the librarians may deal with one hundred loans a day.

Also on Quarter Deck are card rooms, a bar, and the Queen's Room, where you go for music, dancing, and entertainment.

Above — as they say on ships instead of upstairs — Quarter Deck is Upper Deck, where you'll find the largest restaurant — the Mauretania — the theater, and the gambling casino. Children are allowed to play the quarter slot machines, but when the roulette and blackjack games are in progress, no one under eighteen is permitted in the room.

Aft of the casino is the Double Down Room, with its bandstand, dance floor, and large seating area. After dinner the Double Down is a nightclub. During the day all sorts of things go on there: the dance class, bingo, yoga, quizzes and games, arts and crafts. The room's formal name is the Grand Lounge.

If you had been in the Double Room in January 1986, you would have seen history being made. While sailing down the coast of Peru on a round-the-world cruise, QE2's passengers were able to watch the 1986 Super Bowl live via a special satellite hookup.

Walk up the Double Down's horseshoe staircase and you are on Boat Deck, ringed with shops. You can buy clothes, souvenirs, jewelry, toys, games, candy, books, magazines, and electronic gadgets. Forward on Boat Deck is the Queen's Grill, the dining room for people with the most expensive cabins.

Go outside and you'll see how Boat Deck got its name. Suspended over your head are the lifeboats. Boat Deck is the only place on the QE2 where you can walk all the way around outdoors.

You often see joggers on Boat Deck. From a marked spot on the port side to a similar spot to starboard is a fifth of a mile. One way of keeping track of your mileage is to put five coins in your port pocket. Start walking or jogging at the mark on the port side; when you get to the mark on the starboard side, put a coin in your starboard pocket. Do that five times, and you've jogged a mile.

Around Boat Deck, and on Sports Deck above it, are open areas for deck chairs. One of the first things many people do on a ship is pick out a deck chair. The deck steward will put your name on it, and it's yours for the crossing.

The *QE2* amidships, showing Boat Deck. Since 1840, Cunard funnels (smokestacks) have been painted a unique orange-red, originally a mix of ochre and buttermilk.

Some people practically live in their deck chairs — reading, sleeping, pretending to work, eating. If it's cold, the deck steward will wrap you up in blankets. I've often seen people bundled up in deck chairs even when it was raining.

Other activities on Boat Deck and Sports Deck include an electronic golf course, Ping-Pong, paddle tennis, shuffleboard, tetherball, and volleyball.

Near the top of the ship is the playroom, where your sister and other small children are looked after during the day. Not far from the playroom is the kennel. Two kennel maids from England's Bellmead Kennel Maid Training School take care of dogs, cats, gerbils, birds, or whatever pet a passenger is traveling with.

On a recent three-month, round-the-world cruise, two cats shared the kennel and the kennel maids with a duck.

You're not supposed to visit the kennel unless you have a pet aboard. Ask around and try to find someone traveling with an animal. They might let you go with them during owner visiting hours.

The kennel maids are friendly and remarkably unflappable considering the fact that several dogs are usually barking at the same time or chasing each other on their open deck run. If you get to know a dog on board, tell your dining-room waiter. He'll see you get a first-class bone for your next kennel visit.

The bow observation area where you stood at sailing time is a good place from which to see the highest parts of the ship. Above you is the bridge, where the captain and his deck officers use the most advanced equipment, aided by computers, to guide the ship, check weather conditions, and maintain contact with all parts of the ship.

At sailing time a local harbor pilot joins the captain on the bridge. Like a ground controller advising an airplane pilot, the

A dog's life is strictly first class on the QE2. An Irish setter greets a crew member who has come to visit.

harbor pilot uses his knowledge of local conditions such as tides to help the captain take the ship out to sea. The captain, of course, has the final word. He is responsible for the welfare of passengers and crew and of the ship herself.

Once out at sea, the pilot is taken off the ship on a small pilot boat, or sometimes by helicopter or tugboat. A few hours before the QE2 reaches the end of her voyage, an English pilot comes aboard to help guide her into the port of Southampton.

Below the bridge is the communications room, the center for radar, telegraph, telephone, and satellite equipment. On many ships you can reach any direct-dial telephone number in the world in a few minutes. The QE2's daily newspaper is transmitted in six minutes from the Paris newsroom of the *International Herald Tribune.*

The highest part of the ship is the top of the funnel, 204 feet above the base of the keel, the lowest part of the ship.

Forward of the funnel, just aft of the bridge, is the mast. On the mast are navigation lights, one of the ship's whistles, and a closed-circuit television camera pointed at the funnel.

You wouldn't think the funnel would be all that fascinating, but it is to the engineering officers. The officer on watch can keep an eye on a television monitor and see what the smoke coming from the funnel looks like. If it's the wrong color, there may be a problem.

Flying from the top of the mast are flags. At sailing time the QE2 flew the American flag from the highest point because she was sailing from an American port. Below the American flag were three other flags. One was the blue ensign, a flag flown by any British merchant navy ship whose crew includes a certain number of Royal Navy Reserve members. Then came the Cunard house flag, a gold lion on a red field, representing Cunard Line. Finally, there was the red-and-white pilot flag that tells other ships, "I have a pilot aboard." As soon as the QE2 reached the open ocean and the pilot left the ship, the pilot flag was taken down.

Ships all over the world observe an international code of signals. Every ship carries an identical set of flags as well as code books. There is a flag for every letter of the alphabet and one for every number. The signal officer can spell out messages easily read by lookouts on other ships.

On festive occasions it is the custom to "dress ship." All of the signal flags are flown on a line running from stem to stern and up over the mast. The thousands of vessels in New York harbor on July 4, 1986, dressed ship by flying all their flags. It was a grand sight.

The important job of raising and lowering the flags is done by a deck boy. One of a number of teenagers in the crew, the

The *QE2*'s mast at sailing time. Unless she is signaling another vessel, she doesn't fly flags at sea.

deck boy is usually sixteen, right out of three months of sea-school training.

Following a superior's orders, he climbs up to the roof of the bridge, which puts him in a position to manipulate the flags. For almost a century, the roof of a ship's bridge has been called "monkey island," maybe because it takes someone with a monkey's agility to climb up to it.

That's enough for one ship tour on your own. Later on the teen counselor has a group tour scheduled. Then you'll have a chance to spend some time in one of the most fascinating places on the *QE2*, the Computer Learning Center on Two Deck.

Open twenty-four hours every day, the center has rows of IBM personal computers, each with its own printer and paper supply. A box of disks includes a disk on the *QE2*, an introduction to the computer, word processing programs, computer games, and some very advanced software.

There'll be time to see more of the teen club, too. On Upper Deck it has books, video and board games, a jukebox, movies on tape, air hockey, and more to offer.

The rest of your first full day at sea can be spent fitting in as many activities as possible — a teen and preteen Coketail party, a hairdressing demonstration, a tea dance, bingo — or nothing at all. Anything goes at sea.

Sometime during the day your whole family has to see the British immigration officer. It takes only a few minutes and saves time at the landing. He looks at your passports, checks your name off a list, and gives you the stamped landing cards you will need to hand in at the gangway when you leave the ship in Southampton.

Late in the afternoon it's time to dress up. You are traveling in first class. The program that came under your door this morning suggests formal dress for tonight because the captain is hosting a cocktail party for all the first-class passengers. Tomorrow he will meet the other passengers, called transatlantic class.

Ship passengers used to wear formal clothes more than they do now, but people in first class, and some in second class, still like to dress up on the three middle nights of a crossing. You don't dress on the first night because you may not have your luggage yet. And you don't dress on the last night because you'll be getting packed.

Women usually wear evening gowns, some very dressy indeed, or at least dressy short dresses. Men wear evening clothes or dark suits. Boys look right in dark jackets with ties, and girls can wear what they'd wear to a nice restaurant, or go the whole hog and wear a formal gown or dance dress. In first class on the North Atlantic, it's not possible to be too dressed up.

The captain stands just outside the Queen's Room and shakes hands with every single person who comes to the party. Each handshake is photographed. Tomorrow the photos will

Captain Lawrence Portet welcomes Dean Mason to his party. Dean's father, Paul Mason, is a member of the *QE2*'s catering department.

be on display for you to buy — hundreds of pictures of the captain shaking hands. *QE2* Captain Robert Arnott is believed to have the record. He once shook 635 hands in thirty-four minutes.

At the end of the party, just before dinnertime, the cruise director introduces the ship's officers and the captain says a few words. He is always optimistic about the weather.

After dinner and a busy evening, don't forget to go out on deck. You're truly at sea now, and it's probably misty and cool. Last thing before bed, set your clock ahead an hour. The time in England is five hours later than in New York, and you have to catch up.

3

From *Savannah* to *Phoenix*

The reports of my death are greatly exaggerated.

MARK TWAIN

Oceans cover three-quarters of the earth's surface. We humans make our homes on that final quarter — dry land. Living on shore has never stopped people from going to sea. Thousands of years ago, people began to set out across bodies of water in anything that would float — rafts, canoes, and sailboats of every size and shape.

Among those early seagoers were soldiers, merchants, and explorers. Many were colonists hoping to settle in a new country. The Pilgrims who came to America aboard the sailing ship *Mayflower* are a familiar example.

Travelers didn't set off in boats for the fun of it, as they do now. Sea travel under sail was no pleasure trip. The sea was often rough, passengers were crowded together, and journeys took many weeks. When the wind wasn't blowing, sailing ships were at the mercy of the rolling sea. With no wind to drive the ship onward, voyages took even longer.

By 1800 travelers between America and Europe made the long, arduous journey in ships called sailing packets. The ships were given this name because they carried packets of mail.

Those graceful ships that look so romantic in paintings took weeks to cross the ocean. They were crowded and not very clean. There was no such thing as a regular schedule.

Then, in 1817, a group of New York merchants put this announcement in the newspapers:

> In order to furnish frequent and regular conveyance for Goods and Passengers, the subscribers have undertaken to establish a line of vessels between New York and Liverpool [England], to sail from each place on a certain day in every month throughout the year.

The name of the company was the Black Ball Line. Their first ship was the *James Monroe*. The Black Ball Line's owners said that the *James Monroe* would sail at 10:00 A.M. on January 5, 1818, and she did. She crossed the ocean, under sail, in twenty-three days. Every ocean liner on the sea today is a direct descendant of the *James Monroe* and the other Black Ball Line ships.

In the early 1800s, a revolution in ship travel took place. The steam engine was invented, and steam-powered ships soon followed. The principle is simple: Water is heated to boiling in a container called, obviously, a boiler. The water turns to steam, and the steam is used to drive the engine.

For decades, James Watt in England, and several other inventors, had been developing the steam engine. Then an American from Pennsylvania — painter, jewelry maker, and engineer Robert Fulton — built the first commercially successful steamship. His *Clermont* made her maiden voyage on August 17, 1807, sailing the Hudson River between New York City and Albany in thirty-four hours.

You can reasonably say that the *Clermont* led the way to everything from sailing parties to midnight buffets — from the cruise to nowhere to the *Love Boat*.

Although sailing packets would grace the seas for another fifty years, 1819 marked the beginning of their end. On May 24 of that year, *Savannah*, a small paddle-wheel steamer, sailed from her Georgia home port. She crossed the Atlantic and arrived in Liverpool, England, twenty-nine days later. She had been 663 hours at sea, most of the time under sail. She used her fifty-eight-horsepower, one-cylinder steam engine for only eighty-five hours.

The reason *Savannah* didn't steam the whole way was that she was too small to carry enough coal to heat the water needed to make steam for a three-thousand-mile voyage. Another problem was the buildup of salt from the sea water used in the boilers that produced the steam.

Savannah did get up steam when anyone was looking. Most of the people who saw her thought she was on fire. When *Savannah* was sighted off the coast of Ireland, a ship called *Kite* sailed out to her rescue. *Savannah's* captain invited *Kite's* red-faced officers aboard to look her over.

Now, although the little paddle wheeler deserves a place in this story, *Savannah* wasn't really a liner at all. For one thing, she didn't belong to a line. She was the only ship owned by the Savannah Steamship Company.

For another, she didn't carry any passengers. Poor *Savannah*. She had handsome cabins for thirty-two passengers and luxurious lounges with oriental carpets. There were mirrors everywhere. But despite all the advertising her owners did, not a single passenger was willing to make the first power-

The *Savannah*'s funnel puts on a good show, but the steamer crossed the ocean mostly under sail.

driven crossing of what was considered the world's most dangerous ocean.

Savannah's owners tried, and failed, to sell her in England. On she sailed, to Stockholm, Sweden. Karl XIV Johan, king of Sweden and Norway, wanted to buy her. He couldn't afford to, though, because he had just taken over Norway and hadn't finished paying for it yet. Karl did dine aboard and went on a little cruise. Since passengers are treated so royally on cruises, it's only fitting that a king was the first person to go on one.

Still trying to sell *Savannah*, her captain sailed on to Russia.

At last she carried a passenger. He was Thomas Graham, Lord Lynedoch, of England, and he had joined the ship in Stockholm. He had such a good time that he gave the captain an engraved silver tea kettle as a bread-and-butter present.

Lord Lynedoch wasn't just the first steamship passenger. He was a kinsman of John Maxtone-Graham, author of two wonderful books about ocean liners.

The Russian czar didn't buy *Savannah* either. She returned home under sail and never used her steam engines again. A few years later, she ran aground during a storm off the coast of Long Island, New York. Crashing waves quickly put an end to the brave little paddle-wheel pioneer.

In 1819, the same year *Savannah* made her historic voyage, Samuel Cunard, a Canadian businessman, was given a contract by the British government to carry mail in sailing ships from Newfoundland to Boston and Bermuda. The Cunards were Quakers who had left England years before. They had lived for a time in Philadelphia and then settled in British North America, now Nova Scotia, in eastern Canada.

Samuel Cunard was born in Halifax in 1787. His many business interests included banking, lumber, fire insurance, and whaling. He also worked in Boston for three years in the office of a ship broker. Though he came from a working-class background, the resourceful Cunard owned his first ship by the time he was twenty-one.

In 1838, when steamship travel was beginning to grow, the British government was looking for someone to carry the mail by steamship across the Atlantic. Samuel Cunard got that contract, too. He went to Scotland and arranged for four steamships to be built — *Britannia*, *Acadia*, *Caledonia*, and *Columbia*. Those four Cunard ships were the first real ocean liners.

Samuel Cunard's dream was to create what came to be

known as the Atlantic Ferry. He saw no reason why steamships couldn't keep regular schedules like trains and ferryboats.

Britannia wasn't the first ship to cross entirely under power. The *Royal William* made the voyage in 1833. Samuel Cunard was one of her owners. In May 1840 a ship called the *Unicorn* also steamed across the Atlantic.

Earlier, two passenger steamers raced each other across. They were the rival ships *Sirius* and *Great Western*. *Sirius* left Ireland on April 4, 1838, carrying forty passengers. She arrived in New York eighteen days and ten hours later. Her average speed was 6.7 knots.

Knots are mentioned a lot in a book about ships. A knot is a unit of speed across water. On land you talk about miles per hour. At sea a ship's speed is described in knots. When a ship averages eight knots, that means she travels eight nautical miles in an hour. A nautical mile is longer than a land mile. A land mile is 5,280 feet. A nautical mile is about 15 percent longer, or 6076.115 feet (1852 meters).

Three hours after *Sirius* steamed into New York, *Great Western* arrived. The dramatic race between the two ships caused a sensation. Like Aesop's hare, *Great Western* was faster, but came in second. She had made a late start, but she crossed in only fifteen days, five hours, and averaged 8.8 knots. (The *QE2*'s maximum cruising speed is 32.5 knots.)

Those two ships, much larger than *Savannah*, proved it was possible to carry enough coal to cross the ocean under steam. *Sirius* was the first ship to solve the other major obstacle to long-distance steamship travel. She introduced surface condensers, which turned sea water into fresh water and kept salt from accumulating in the boilers.

Sirius made only one other crossing. *Great Western* stayed on the Atlantic for many years. But Samuel Cunard gets the credit for starting the first real ocean liners.

On July 4, 1840, Cunard's first liner, *Britannia*, made her maiden voyage, with Samuel Cunard among her sixty-three passengers. She crossed in fourteen days, eight hours.

Samuel Cunard started the first steamship line, but *Sirius* and *Great Western* started something else — racing across the Atlantic. For the next hundred years, most steamship companies wanted to have the fastest ships on the ocean.

Newspapers and shipowners started talking about something called the Blue Ribbon of the Atlantic, an award for the fastest crossing.

There certainly was never a real ribbon pinned like a medal on the winning captain, but whatever ship held the honor often flew a blue streamer from her mast.

Britannia, the first ocean liner. Two hundred and seven feet long, she could carry 115 passengers.

Competition for the Blue Ribbon was fierce on what has been called the frantic Atlantic. Paying passengers wanted to travel on the fastest ship, and merchants wanted to ship their goods the fastest way. Some ship owners weren't all that safety conscious.

One man who cared more for speed than safety was Edward K. Collins, a very successful American packet-boat operator. The U.S. Congress gave him a lot of money to build steamers that would rival those of the Cunard Line.

One of the Collins Line ships, *Pacific,* was the first to cross in under ten days. She took the Blue Ribbon for the United States.

Pacific, steaming along too fast, as usual, disappeared in an ice field in 1856. Two years earlier, another Collins liner, *Arctic,* was going too fast in a fog. Under Collins's orders, her captain was after records. *Arctic* ran into another ship and sank, taking with her Edward Collins's wife, daughter, and son. Collins went bankrupt a few years later.

Despite such tragedies, passengers loved the idea of the Blue Ribbon. Steamship lines officially denied that they were competing for speed records. Editorials in the papers called the race reckless. It was a fact, though, that whatever ship held the Blue Ribbon made the front pages and had big profits in passengers and freight. British ships held the record for years. Later, German, French, and Italian companies all had Blue Ribbon liners.

For one hundred years after the Collins Line went out of business, no U.S. ship held the Blue Ribbon. Then, in July 1952, the liner *United States* broke the eastbound record on her maiden voyage. On the way back home, she broke the westbound record. Her Blue Ribbon time was three days, ten hours, and forty minutes. That's an average of 35.39 knots. On July 6–7, she steamed 868 sea miles in twenty-four hours.

By then there was a real trophy. An Englishman named Harold Hales had always wanted to present a trophy for the fastest Atlantic ship crossing. The Hales Trophy, all one hundred pounds and four feet of it, was first presented by Mr. Hales to the Italian ship *Rex* in 1935. Later that year the prize was won by the magnificent French liner *Normandie.*

The *Queen Mary*, one of Cunard's most popular liners, beat all previous records. Cunard has always refused to be a part of speed contests, however, and never carried the trophy aboard the *Mary*. After 1952 the record times made by the *United States* were considered unbeatable.

Since the *United States* went out of service in 1969, the Hales Trophy has been exhibited at the American Merchant Marine Academy Museum on Long Island, outside of New York City. The trophy is valuable as well as remarkable to look at. The gold and silver alone are worth well over one hundred thousand dollars.

Two more attempts have been made to break the Atlantic speed record, but not by liners. In 1985 nine Englishmen sailed from New York, in a sixty-five-foot speedboat called *Virgin Atlantic Challenger*. The organizer, and a major sponsor as well as part of the crew, was Richard Bransom, owner of Virgin Atlantic Airways. Bransom is well-known in England as a pop records and airline tycoon.

If *Challenger* had beaten the record, there would have been a big row. Both the Blue Ribbon and the Hales Trophy are understood to be for passenger ships. *Challenger* was a small speedboat with two bunks and no bathroom, hardly a luxury liner. Jokes were made about one of the crew being the designated passenger.

Frank Braynard is curator of the American Merchant Marine Academy Museum and a renowned ship historian. He was quoted as saying that the museum wouldn't give Bransom the trophy if *Challenger* set a new record. The question didn't arise in 1985 because *Challenger* hit some debris and sank, ninety miles short of her goal.

In June 1986 Mr. Bransom tried again. He and his redesigned *Virgin Atlantic Challenger II* left New York with a crew of six on June 29. Three days, eight hours, and thirty-one minutes later they arrived safely. Refueling stops were made along the way. A British Royal Air Force plane even dropped fuel to them. *Challenger II*'s time took two hours and nine minutes off the previous record set by the *United States.*

Challenger II has the Atlantic speed record, but she doesn't have the Hales Trophy. Mr. Braynard said: "No way are we going to give it up. The trophy is our number one exhibit and meant for an ocean liner, not a toy boat."

Samuel Cunard would have disapproved of all this racing about the Atlantic. Right from the start, he said his goal was to provide safe, reliable, fast weekly service between Europe and America. He told the masters of his ships that there would be "no racing, rivalry or risk taking." The line's motto was Speed, Comfort, and Safety.

Cunard's ideas were received with great enthusiasm. When *Britannia* arrived in Boston on her maiden voyage in 1840, thousands of people made up a parade on the spot. A banquet for a thousand people was given, and Mr. Cunard received eighteen hundred dinner invitations and several marriage proposals. The banquet marked the first time women attended a public dinner in Boston.

Twenty-three hundred Bostonians chipped in to buy Cunard a five-thousand-dollar solid silver cup. That cup is on the *QE2* today. It's the first thing you see when you walk into the Columbia Restaurant.

Samuel Cunard ran his shipping company with skill and charm for twenty-five years. He died in April 1865, two weeks after Abraham Lincoln was killed.

The Cunard Line has stuck to its founder's principles. No Cunard passenger has ever died through the fault of the line, a remarkable record.

In the early days, not everyone was pleased with Cunard ships. Sailing to the United States for an author tour in 1842, Charles Dickens complained steadily. It's only fair to point out that the famous author of *David Copperfield* and *Great Expectations* crossed on the *Britannia* in the winter, on one of the worst crossings on record.

In his *American Notes* Dickens described his crossing in detail, and he did enjoy some of it. But Mr. Dickens had expected a much bigger cabin. He said it was as hard to find a place for his wife's luggage as it would be to put a giraffe in a flowerpot.

The author's sailing party sounds like going-away parties on many ships today. At one point he and his friends watched deck hands "taking in the milk." Ships carried live cows in those days.

Dickens often went up on deck at night. "This is a very striking time on shipboard," he wrote. "It never ceased to have a peculiar interest and charm for me. . . . the rushing water, plainly heard, but dimly seen; the broad white glistening track that follows in the vessel's wake; the men on the look-out; . . . the melancholy sighing of the wind."

Dickens could have written those words today.

During a bad storm, however, Charles Dickens said, "I found myself on deck . . . holding on to something. I don't know what. I think it was the boatswain; or it may have been the pump; or possibly the cow. I could not even make out which was the sea, and which the sky, for the horizon . . . was flying wildly about, in all directions."

After the storm, normal shipboard life went on. Any ship passenger today would recognize Mr. Dickens's description of the gossipy little world of a ship at sea. Everyone talked about everyone else. The smallest oddities made a sensation. "News!" Mr. Dickens said. "A dozen murders on shore would lack the interest of these slight incidents at sea."

None of the early liners were very comfortable. There were no stabilizers, no medicine for seasickness. There wasn't much to do either. The cruise director hadn't been invented yet. Passengers entertained themselves, sometimes lavishly.

Many famous people traveled on ships. The famous ones, and those who could afford it, traveled in cabins — in a central section of the ship called cabin class, or first class, and sometimes first cabin or second cabin. Everyone else went in steerage — big, open areas where passengers were crowded together. It was called steerage because in the beginning it was in the stern near the steering gear.

First-class passengers got most of the space and all of the

Between decks, immigrants ate and slept without any luxuries while crossing the ocean in 1844.

comfort. Steerage brought in the greatest profits for the shipping lines. From 1815 to 1921, thirty million people left their homes and came to settle in the United States. Most of them came by ship from western and northern Europe.

Conditions on the sailing packets and early liners were awful. Many people died. Then, in the early 1850s, England's Inman Line began to upgrade the old immigrant quarters. Living conditions were better, and voyages were shorter.

By the end of the century, steerage had its own dining rooms. Before that, steerage passengers brought food and cooked it themselves. Bathrooms were added, as well as lounges, and even some semiprivate cabins.

Then, in 1921, the U.S. government passed a law that severely limited immigration. The vast wave of immigrants dried up almost overnight. Steamship companies had to fill their ships in other ways. From 1921 on, most ocean liner passengers were Americans. Steerage was upgraded into second- and third-class sections. Most liners had three classes, and some even four.

Liners had special rooms for children, who were hidden away out of sight of the grown-ups. Only in the past ten or fifteen years have shipping lines begun making ships appealing to whole families.

From the time she made her first crossing in 1969, the *QE2* has given special attention to its young passengers. They have a children's costume party — called the children's fancy dress — in the Double Room. Children are welcome in the dining rooms and all over the ship.

On the old ships, the classes were completely separated. You could look at a deck plan and know that beyond a wall was another class, but try to get in there. The *France* went into service in 1962 with two sections that were closed off most of

An early attempt to amuse young ocean travelers — the children's social director, aboard the German liner *Imperator* in 1912.

the time. She even had a children's dining room, tucked away.

Seven years later the *QE2* became the first completely open ship. On transatlantic crossings she has two classes with their own dining rooms, lounges, and bars. Everyone can go every- where, though — no walled-off areas.

On cruises the *QE2* has only one class. All the dining rooms serve the same menu, instead of offering fancier dishes as the first-class dining rooms do on crossings. Cruises are usually less expensive than crossings. Today, most ships do far more cruising than crossing and are one class all the time.

Ships have changed in many ways since 1840. Propellers replaced paddle wheels, and engines were improved. New materials and modern building methods completely altered the way ships were constructed.

Ships began to use oil instead of coal to heat their boilers. This saved time, for one thing. Pumping in oil takes much less time than shoveling in coal. As coal was burned up, a ship became lighter and rode higher in the water. A light ship, riding on top of the waves instead of down in them, gives a much bumpier ride. When an oil tank is emptied, water can be pumped in to keep the weight the same.

By the 1890s ships began to have electric lights. By 1907, Cunard's *Mauretania*, the first of many great express liners, was crossing in five days, only a few hours slower than the *QE2* today. For another fifty years, ocean liners, ever more luxurious, were the only way to cross the Atlantic. Then came the jet plane, offering fast, cheap travel, and passengers abandoned ships in droves.

Instead of enjoying comfortable cabins, leisurely meals and plenty of them, swimming, parties, dancing, meeting new people with time to make friends, millions of people traveled by jet. Jets didn't offer luxury or comfort, but they got people to Europe in hours instead of days.

Ship buffs sighed and sighed and said the end was near. One of the sighers was John Maxtone-Graham. In his entertaining and fascinating book about ocean liners, *The Only Way to Cross*, he talks sadly about the end of a great era.

"The reports of my death are greatly exaggerated," Mark Twain cabled the Associated Press when it printed his obituary. The death of ocean liners was exaggerated, too.

Today, passenger ships have never been so healthy. And no one is happier about it than Mr. Maxtone-Graham. In his 1985 *Liners to the Sun*, he points out the differences — and similarities — between old and new ships. He also believes that though ship travel is different, it's better.

You can still cross the Atlantic by ship. You can also travel the world's oceans and rivers, something that was not possible until recently. Liners go to the Antarctic, and to within nine hundred miles of the North Pole.

Ships visit almost every country with a coast. You can sail two thousand miles up the Amazon, often without seeing the shore at all, or take a Mississippi paddle wheeler as far as Minnesota. You can go by ship to ports in more than thirty states. Ships travel across the top of Alaska through the Northwest Passage, and through the Saint Lawrence River to Montreal. Rhine steamers sail through Holland, France, Germany, and Switzerland.

The spring 1987 travel section of the *New York Times* listed seventy-three shipping companies that would send information about their cruises. Many have toll-free numbers. I've called dozens of them, and enjoy looking through the brochures and daydreaming.

In the spring of 1986, the American Ship Building Company announced plans for the first passenger ships to be built in U.S. shipyards in thirty years. The ships will make cruises in the Hawaiian Islands.

Twenty-five new cruise ships have gone into service since 1982, and over a dozen more are planned for 1987 and 1988. Cunard has so much faith in the future of crossing and cruising that it converted the *QE2* from steam to diesel power during a six-month refit in the winter of 1986–87. Before the refit the *QE2*'s mileage was a whopping twenty-nine feet to the gallon. Now she gets twice that footage using diesel fuel.

The most remarkable of the new ships is still on the drawing boards. She will be called *Phoenix*, after the mythical bird that rose from its own ashes.

Knut Kloster is the man behind *Phoenix*. His company is Norwegian Caribbean Lines, and he started the cruise ship

The *Rotterdam*, near the top of the world, in Glacier Bay, Alaska.

boom in Miami. He also rescued the beautiful liner *France,* the longest liner ever built, after the French Line took her out of service in 1974. Mr. Kloster turned her into the *Norway,* and now she's in regular service between Florida and the Bahamas.

The *Phoenix* would be the largest passenger ship — by a lot. She would be 1,200 feet long, weigh a quarter of a million pounds, and carry 5,000 passengers. Most of them would have outside cabins with terraces. There would be a theater seating 2,000 people and six or seven restaurants.

I hope the *Phoenix* is built. Even if she isn't, she symbolizes the faith of Mr. Kloster, Cunard, and dozens of other shipping companies in the future of passenger liners.

Ocean liners have survived wars, skyrocketing oil prices, and the cheap travel offered by jets. Millions of people are rediscovering ship travel, the best vacation bargain anyone, especially families, can find.

Now, more than ever before, travelers can enjoy what John Maxtone-Graham calls "that magical passenger life on board."

4

Day Three

"What is the use of a book," thought Alice, "without pictures or conversation?"

Lewis Carroll, *Alice's Adventures in Wonderland*

Shipboard life has much in common with Wonderland and the world Alice found through the looking glass. You can meet a great variety of characters, a lot of eating goes on, and there is as much conversation as even Alice could hope for.

Most of the passengers and crew members are friendly. Some may be a bit peculiar, and some are both friendly and odd. Chatting them up, as the English say, is one of the pleasures of ship travel.

A ship — any ship, anywhere — is a world of its own, self-sufficient, detached from reality. I've always thought of the end of a voyage as going back to real life, and sometimes wished I didn't have to.

Even when I'm reluctant to end a trip, I'm aware that a crossing's limits are part of its charm. After all, in five days, how lazy can you get, or how spoiled, or how fat?

Indulge yourself. Have your fill of swimming or Ping-Pong

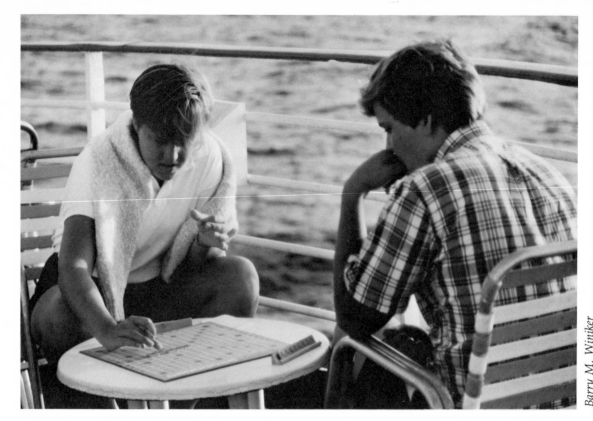

Making friends.

or playing with a computer. Lie in your deck chair all day and let your deck steward wrap blankets around you and bring you trays of pastry. You don't even have to think about tipping for all that service. On ships tipping is done in lump sums on the last day.

Talk to people. Be nosy. Ask questions. The best conversation starter on a ship is, "Are you having a good crossing?" People love to talk about themselves, and you'll learn a great deal about travel and ships by asking other passengers how their crossing is going.

A ship is a perfect place for an outgoing, social sort of person. What may not be quite so obvious is that the contained, limited world of a ship is ideal for shy people. It's a great place to practice not being shy.

Speaking as an ex-shy person, I know how hard it can be to make friends in a new school or class or neighborhood. If you're prone to saying dumb things — putting your foot in your mouth — you may feel it's better not to say much at all. A closed mouth gathers no feet.

But if you spend a five-day crossing with your foot in your mouth, so what? At the end, it's back to reality, and you won't have to see any of those people ever again — unless you want to. It's not as if you'll come to class on Monday and there they'll be.

I believe that more people are shy than are naturally outgoing. Many of the passengers and crew — young and not so young — will be glad to have the conversational ice broken. The person at the next video game, or leaning on the rail near you, or swimming lonely laps in the pool will probably be grateful to have you grin and say, "Are you having a good crossing?" Try it.

Eating is one of life's best social activities, and on a ship you seldom eat alone. Much good conversation happens over meals. You can, though I don't necessarily advise it, spend a whole five-day crossing doing almost nothing except eating.

Start by having the early-bird tea and rolls on deck at 7:00 A.M. Then ask your stewardess to bring you juice and a doughnut while you are back in your cabin reading the daily program. She may have a few minutes for chatting.

Then you can go with your family to the dining room and order something you won't be able to get later at the breakfast buffet — pancakes, perhaps. Or be daring and have a kipper. Kippers are smoked and salted fish. English people like to have them for breakfast.

While you're practicing not being shy, you can also experiment with food. A ship is the perfect place to try food you would never think of ordering at home.

For one thing, all meals are included in the price of your ticket, so no matter how much you eat or how often, it doesn't cost any more. For another, the variety is enormous, and the steward will gladly give you tiny servings so you can try different things.

After breakfast in the dining room, nip aft on Quarter Deck, where until 9:45 a huge buffet breakfast is served. I like the way the English pronounce buffet; it rhymes with *huffy*.

The breakfast buffet is served cafeteria-style. Trays are big enough for cereal, fruit, juice, rolls and toast, sausage, eggs, bacon, jam, and milk. Most people sit at tables near the pool under the Magrodome. I take my tray outside, where I can look out past the stern and see the wake. While you eat, you can watch people down on One Deck swimming or larking about.

By the time you've finished the fourth breakfast, you have time to jog around the deck for forty-five minutes before you are due at your deck chair for the next meal.

At 11:00 you should be in your deck chair ready for an ancient ship tradition called eleven o'clock bouillon. The deck steward will offer you bouillon, tea, or coffee, all brought to you on a tray. Or you can have a soft drink. The steward follows the bouillon with a tray of crackers and cookies, just the thing to tide you over until lunch.

When a ship is cruising, there is usually an elaborate buffet near the pool. But on a crossing of the Atlantic, lunch is served only in the dining room, except for hot dogs and other snacks near the One Deck pool. On a cruise you can have lunch in both places.

Bingo is played every afternoon in the Double Room just before time to dress for dinner. Tea — your next meal — is served, and with it come terrific pastries. I recommend the little raspberry tarts. If you don't play bingo, or are too late for tea, wander along the port side aft of the Queen's Room. Sometimes raspberry tarts from the Queen's Room tea are left sitting by themselves. No one will mind if you have one or two.

Dinner gives you the best chance to experiment. Try the caviar. You may find it too salty and fishy tasting, although really good caviar, like that served in first class, is quite mild and delicious.

An exotic way to eat caviar is in blini, little Russian pancakes about two inches across. The steward will put a blini on your plate, spoon caviar on it, add a dollop of sour cream and another blini, and pour melted butter over everything.

When I talked to eight-year-old Kristina Hicks, who lives in Saint Charles, Illinois, she was having a great crossing. She was in the Ping-Pong tournament. At mealtime she was eating her way through the menu. "You can have anything you like," Kristy said, "and it's all free. I usually get desserts that flame."

Try a flaming dessert. The table captain will wheel a big cart to your table and start heating up little pancakes in butter. He'll squeeze oranges into the pan, pour orange liqueur and some brandy on top, and then set the whole thing on fire. It goes up with a great swoosh. (I once saw some waiters hastily move the cart because it was under the ceiling sprinkler. The spout of fire would have set off the sprinkler, soaking the people at the next table.) When the flame has gone out, you are served with heavenly crêpes suzette.

The captain will also flame cherries for you — cherries

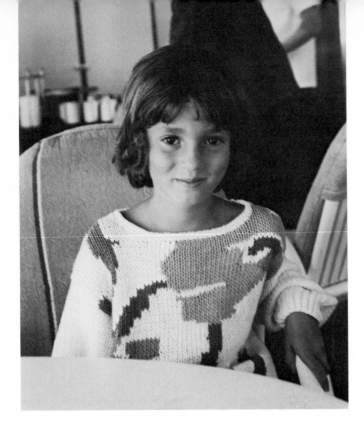

At dinner Kristy always orders a flaming dessert.

jubilee — and pour them over ice cream. Talk it over with the table captain. Like Kristy, you might be able to have something served in flames every night.

Some people eat their cherries straight. I was at a table once with Marion Stoney and her parents, from Tennessee. Fifteen-year-old Marion mentioned that she could tie a cherry stem in a knot in her mouth.

She picked her stem carefully and then sat there with a lot of activity going on behind her closed mouth. While I stared, fascinated, I realized her parents were staring, too. This was a skill of their daughter's they didn't know she had.

A few minutes later — presto! Out of Marion's mouth came a cherry stem, neatly knotted.

After dinner and the evening's entertainments, there is still more food available. Under the Magrodome, people are eating sandwiches and cake to the accompaniment of disco music and flashing lights. Take a sandwich out on deck and eat it under the biggest sky you've ever seen.

On *QE2* cruises a huge buffet is served in the Columbia Restaurant at midnight. Most cruise ships have fancy midnight buffets.

If you get peckish — another British word — during the night, ring for the night steward. He'll be glad to bring you a sandwich to get you through until you can have your four breakfasts.

By the time you have spent a day eating, you will have noticed that some of the waiters are very young. If you chat up some of them, you'll find that in England many people who are not going to a university leave school at sixteen. Those who want to work on ships spend three months of concentrated training at the National Sea Training College in London.

Peter Skelcher, now in his twenties, started sea school when he was sixteen. His father, Robin, has been with Cunard for over thirty years.

Since Peter Skelcher started on the *QE2*, he has worked in many parts of the ship.

At sea school everyone takes a week-long fire-fighting course and spends ten days learning about lifeboats and other survival techniques. After that they go into different sections depending on what part of the merchant navy they want to be in.

Peter wanted to be on passenger ships, working in the catering department. Of the thousand crew members on the QE2 each crossing, three hundred run the ship — in the engine room, on the bridge, doing maintenance. The other seven hundred are on the catering staff — everyone who deals with the passengers.

Peter spent eight weeks in sea school learning how to make beds, wash dishes, clean, tend bar, and serve in the cabins, public rooms, and dining rooms.

For three of those weeks, he studied cookery, as cooking is called in England. "The first two weeks," he told me, "you do training cookery, basic stuff. Then the third week we cooked for everyone in the sea school.

"It's a pretty good level of food, actually. Amazing, really, what you can learn in two weeks of intensive cooking. It's just the basics. They expect you to learn the fancy stuff when you go into the ship's kitchens."

Peter started out as a *commis* waiter in the Princess Grill of the QE2. *Commis* is a French word for clerk or shop assistant. On ships a *commis* waiter is a waiter-in-training. Many people call them "jam boys" because at breakfast they push around the cart with the jam jars on it. Jam boys slice smoked salmon, serve the egg and onion for the caviar, and do dozens of other jobs. Peter Skelcher has also been a public room and cabin steward and a barman.

Most of the crew I've talked with like to work where the passengers are, rather than behind the scenes. "I like to meet people," Robin Skelcher, Peter's father, says, "and there's more variety."

The crew seems to feel the same way most passengers do about the social life aboard ship. Talking to crew members gives you a peek into a very different life-style. Most of them are on the ship for several months and home on leave for a few weeks. While at sea they work most of the time, the equivalent of a double shift.

When the working time is nearly up, the crew starts getting homesick. *QE2* crew members have a phrase for the feeling they get when they're nearing the English Channel and almost home. If a waiter gets your order wrong or drops something or just seems to be daydreaming, you'll hear someone say, "He's got a bad case of the channels."

You've been eating internationally, and talking to crew members from other countries. In the teen club and around the ship, you'll find people to chat with from all around the world.

When I was researching this book, I was on a crossing with kids from the United States, England, Germany, Italy, and France. And those were just the regulars in the club. Julie

Water volleyball knows no age limits, as long as your chin is above water.

Grist, the estimable counselor on that crossing, speaks several languages and knows all the best tricks for getting people together, even when they don't speak the same language.

I asked Julie if all those different languages and cultures made for problems. She grinned at me. "Kids are kids," said Julie.

You may assume that on an English ship you'll understand everything the English crew and passengers say. Not necessarily.

If you say to the deck steward, "Good morning, how are you?" and he says, "Mustn't grumble," it's pretty clear what he means. But suppose you hear a mother say to her young child, "Now you stop that wingeing." *Winge* is a wonderful English word for whine. A winger is a whiner. An English-woman once told me about her son's first sports day at school. He called her afterward and said, "I lost every race, Mummy, but I didn't winge."

There are four months' worth of things to do in five days, but you could do worse than spend them chatting and eating and reading in your deck chair.

By the third day, you're an old hand. You know your way around, you've made friends among the passengers and crew. Now is a good time to investigate a few places not everyone sees.

5

Seventy-Nine Thousand Eggs, One Disc Jockey...

"Please sir, I want some more."

CHARLES DICKENS, *Oliver Twist*

Ocean liners are often called floating hotels. Exploring some of the ship's special places will help show what is involved in stocking all the food and other supplies needed on a voyage, and how varied a crew is necessary to make a voyage go smoothly.

The kitchens are a good place to start. Hotels on land bring in new supplies every day, and a big hotel has a huge amount of storage room. If a hotel runs out of something, the manager can call up a wholesaler or send someone down to the fish market or the nearest dairy.

On a ship at sea, the hotel manager can't run to the market or borrow from the neighbors, and there is limited closet space. The hotel manager and the staff must know exactly what they will need for each voyage, where to order it, and how to get it to the ship and stored away during the few hours the ship is in port.

The *QE2* isn't completely restocked every time she docks. Supplies of frozen and canned foods, and staples such as flour, sugar, and other dried and bottled items can last from trip to trip, as storage space permits.

Fresh food is brought aboard at every port, as well as replacements for stock that is getting low. Local goodies are often added, too. Nearly 150 people work in the *QE2*'s kitchens. The bakers — there are sixteen of them — get up long before dawn to start making bread and rolls and pastries. Cooks roast hundreds of chickens at the same time. Kitchen helpers chop bushels of onions and cut up other vegetables on what looks like acres of chopping blocks.

You can watch cakes being decorated — ships are very big on birthdays and other special occasions.

In one part of the kitchen you can see some of the seventy-nine thousand eggs brought on board for a five-day crossing. It's hard to imagine seventy-nine thousand eggs.

There's also a mile of sausages. If you took a mile-long string of sausages and ran it from the bow up over the mast and down to the stern, you could loop them around the stern flagstaff and run them back up the mast and to the bow all over again. And then once again. You could have three rows of sausages, dressing the ship like signal flags.

Or how about this statistic? The *QE2* carries enough ice cream to make 24,000 ice cream cones. The ship also carries 2,500 gallons of milk, almost 10,000 jars of jam, 3,000 pounds of cheese, 22,000 pounds of fresh fruit, and 5,000 pounds of chicken.

There are 50,000 tea bags and 150 pounds of caviar. Let's not forget either the babies or the dogs. The *QE2* stocks 600 jars of baby food and 50 pounds of dog biscuits.

While exploring off-the-beaten-track parts of the ship, you

probably won't want to visit the efficient hospital with doctors, nurses, a dentist, and a complete operating room. But you might ask to see where the disc jockey works. The ship's radio has programs on all day long. These include several hours of recorded music as well as live interviews with celebrity travelers and crew members. The disc jockey also plays record requests.

Other occupations represented among the ship's crew are cruise staff men and women, who organize passenger entertainment and activities on crossings and cruises; nannies in the nursery; printers who put out the ship's bulletins; mechanics, plumbers, electricians, and carpenters; gambling casino employees; dancers, musicians, and other entertainers; exercise specialists, beauticians, florists, bartenders, and glory-hole stewards.

Glory hole is an old name for the place where the stewards sleep. *Steward* is an even older word. It goes back to early English words meaning a watcher or guardian of the house. Stewards on ships, and on planes, watch out for the passengers. A glory-hole steward is the stewards' steward.

One of the most popular teen club activities is called "autograph hunt." It takes you to many parts of the ship and lets you meet people in all sorts of ship jobs.

"Autograph hunt" is a day-long competition. Everyone who enters is given a list of thirty shipboard occupations. Contestants have to find the people doing those jobs and get them to sign the entry form. You put your name and cabin number on the bottom, turn it in to the teen club and hope you've won.

You must find, among others: a sailor, a swimming pool attendant, a hotel officer, a bedroom steward, a Double Room steward, a deck officer, a playroom attendant, two people from the beauty parlor, a flower shop person, the disc jockey, three members of the cruise staff, two musicians, two people from the shops, a photographer, two entertainers, the entertainments manager, the purser, two waiters, a bartender, a petty officer, and a sports director.

When you're looking for ship's officers, it's helpful to know a little about their insignia. What you learn will apply to most of the ships you travel on.

You can tell by the stripes on an officer's shoulders and sleeves what his or her rank and department are. The captain's uniform has four gold stripes against a black background. On white dress uniforms the stripes are on a black epaulet.

No one is more important than the captain, but there are other officers who wear four stripes. The chief engineer also wears four gold stripes, but they are on a purple background.

When the liner *Titanic* sank in 1912, she took all of the engineering officers with her. To honor them for staying at their posts, King George V of England decreed that the engineers' color would forever be royal purple. So when you see an officer whose stripes are on a purple background, you'll know the officer is a member of the engineering department.

On many ships only the captain and chief engineer are four-stripers. On the *QE2* the staff captain, closest in rank to the captain, is also a four-striper. So is the deputy chief engineer, the hotel manager, and the deputy hotel manager.

Hotel managers and all of the personnel who serve in the huge catering department of the ship wear their gold stripes on a white background.

The purser, who sees to the comfort and welfare of passengers, also wears his or her stripes on a white field. If you meet an officer with gold stripes on red, she or he is the doctor; if the stripes are on a green field, you have found the radio officer.

Staff Captain D. A. Carr and his daughter Alison.

What does the crew of an ocean liner do in the little spare time they have? In their quarters are their own social areas. In addition, the videocassette craze has come to the ship, and many of the crew have videocassette recorders in their cabins. They borrow movies from the ship's library or bring their own on board. Many of the crew ask their families to tape special television shows. Then they bring the tapes on board after they've been home on leave.

Now and then crew members go in for more adventurous

activities. Two friends of mine put a message in a cheese cracker jar and threw it overboard late one night.

I should warn you right now that it's no use trying this yourself unless you can get a crew member to help. If you just toss a bottle over the side, it will be pulled back aboard by the speed of the ship and maybe hurt someone, or else it will break. But a crew member might toss a bottle overboard for you from a special crew section on the stern. That way it can be dropped into the wake and carried swiftly away from the ship.

My friends put their names and Southampton addresses in the cheese cracker jar. Four or five months later, they got an answer. A man wrote from the Aran Islands, in the Atlantic Ocean off the west coast of Ireland.

The man had seen the gleam of white paper in the jar as it rested in some seaweed near the pier on the tiny island where he lives. He had a neighbor write the letter for him. My friends wrote back to him, sending menus, brochures, and other ship information, and telling him about their jobs on board. They heard from him again and learned that he has a small farm and owns a donkey.

Someone else I know in the crew threw a dozen soda bottles overboard one day. After nine months he had a reply from one of them. He's still waiting to hear from the other eleven.

An optimist aboard the *Fairsea* entrusts a letter to the ocean currents.

Barry M. Winiker

6

Day Four

The storm shall not wake thee, nor shark over-
take thee,
Asleep in the arms of the slow-swinging seas.

RUDYARD KIPLING, *The Jungle Book*

The fourth day is a good one for staring out to sea. You're at home on the ship now, and you know what activities you're interested in. You have a routine of sorts. At this point during your crossing, I hope the ocean gives you a chance to experience one of its stormy moods.

As for seasickness, not to worry, as the English say. It's seldom a problem on today's liners.

Until recently, no one on an ocean liner ever talked about seasickness — except the passengers, of course. Nothing was put in the ship's daily bulletins or news sheets. Seasickness is a highly suggestible ailment. The worst thing you can do is talk about it.

Only when a storm was approaching did a discreet little notice appear saying that an anti–motion sickness injection was available in the doctor's office twenty-four hours a day.

Now all that has changed. In the *QE2 Times* these days there is a regular mention of the newest superinjection. The old injection used to put people to sleep for many hours. Today you can have the shot, rest briefly, and feel fine for the whole trip.

The *QE2* doctor I talked to doesn't think much of over-the-counter antihistamine-based remedies for children, though they're all right for adults. Such products may make an adult sleepy, but children sometimes have the opposite reaction and become overexcited.

By way of showing how psychological seasickness is, the doctor told me that in stormy weather children usually don't get sick. "Go up to the playroom in a storm," he said. "It's high up, where there's much more motion, but it'll be full of kids playing, perfectly happy."

He added that whereas he has been sick himself on other ships big and small, he has never been sick on the *QE2*, his home.

My favorite of the new remedies is powdered gingerroot capsules, available from health food stores. Recent research at universities has shown gingerroot to be a very effective motion sickness preventative. I've certainly used it successfully in some pretty rough weather.

Whatever you and your family decide to use, with the approval of your family doctor, by all means take it from the beginning if you're afraid of getting seasick. The remedies are harmless in limited use, so why be sorry later?

I always take something, lately gingerroot, starting when we're still tied up at the dock. I don't know if I get seasick — I've crossed the Atlantic forty times, once in a hurricane — and I don't want to find out.

There are happier experiences than seasickness that are

unique to ocean travel. A cracking good storm is definitely one of them.

The North Atlantic is famous for rough weather at any time of the year. Passenger ships abandon it entirely during the winter. But even in July and August there's usually at least a day when you have no doubt you are on a ship at sea.

One of the early indications of a storm brewing is a louder, more rhythmic creaking sound throughout the ship. Early in the trip you've probably noticed that the ship creaks a little.

The sound is gentle and comforting at first. But it may seem less than reassuring when a storm is brewing and the creaking is louder — creeeak . . . creeeeeak. Believe me, you want it to creak. Ships are built to be flexible, so their parts give in rough weather instead of snapping. The creaking sound is a friendly sound.

I've often heard people say how well they sleep on a ship, with its gentle rolling and that comforting creaking noise. But if the sea really gets rough, you may find the rolling isn't so gentle. Then even the stabilizer fins don't completely prevent the ship from rolling from side to side. In bad weather a ship also pitches — the bow dips down, rises up, dips down again. No one has ever invented a way to keep a ship from pitching.

Nowadays sophisticated technical instruments give accurate information about the location of storms at sea. In many cases the ship's course can be altered to avoid them. But not always.

During a storm you may find your things falling around. When I was on the *Kungsholm* during a hurricane, I ended up keeping a bowl of flowers in the wastebasket, with my clock and various small rolling objects on the floor beside it.

I doubt you'll actually fall out of bed, though if you do, just get back in. Here's my favorite falling-out-of-bed story. A crew friend of mine on the *QE2* sleeps in a lower bunk with a big storage drawer under it. Once, in a storm, the ship rolled and the drawer slid open just as my friend rolled out of bed. He rolled right into the drawer. Fortunately, it didn't slide back with him inside it.

If a storm has come up in the night, you'll find some changes when you go above. Crew members may have "put the ropes up." That means setting posts with ropes in all the open spaces, so there is always something to hang on to. They look just like the ropes you line up between at the movies or in a bank.

It isn't necessary to put up many ropes, though. Look around any ship and you'll see that there are very few big open places. Almost anywhere on a liner you are within grabbing range of a bannister, railing, chair, table, or something.

In a severe storm you won't be able to get out on deck. The doors will be blocked. The danger isn't so much that you'll fall overboard as that you might slip on the spray-washed deck or be knocked over by the wind. You could sprain an ankle and no one would know you were there.

But if it's just a matter of what is called "a good sea running" — waves maybe thirty feet or so — you can go out on deck to watch the sea and the wind-driven spray, and the great ship moving safely through.

It's wonderful out on deck in a storm. You'll need a coat, something for your head, and shoes with spongy soles. Stand on one of the highest decks.

You'll find you can stand on deck for hours in a storm, just watching the constantly changing sea, the wake boiling out astern, and the gray, angry waves falling over on themselves in crashes of foam.

If you get cold, I know a warm place. It is close to a big deck chair area on the QE2's Sports Deck. Companionways, as stairs are called on ships, lead up there from Boat Deck. Nearby, out

Aboard the *Kungsholm* during Hurricane Dolly, a boy shouts for pure joy.

on the open deck, are two white metal cubes about four feet square. They seem to serve no purpose at all.

Stand beside those cubes on a cold day and you'll find the air is ten or fifteen degrees warmer than in any other place on deck. Look closely at the cubes and you'll see why. Deep slits are cut into the metal sides. They are the exhaust vents from the laundry ten decks below. Nice, warm steam, sometimes smelling of starch or bleach, comes up through the vents and warms the area by the cubes.

From the highest decks you can check out the swimming pools. In a real storm the pools are drained, or at least covered over with netting so no one falls in. In a fairly heavy sea, swimming isn't allowed, but the pools are left open. You can watch the pool water sloshing back and forth, and sometimes splashing over the sides. Waves in the pools tend to build up like the tides — slosh, slosh, slosh, whooooosh.

In a mild sea, when you are still allowed to swim, don't miss the experience. Sometimes you're swimming uphill, sometimes the waves in the pool carry you effortlessly from one end to another. The niftiest sensation is just lying in the water in the middle. The salt water buoys you up, the ship's motion makes waves in the pool, and you are rocked or maybe even sloshed a bit with no effort on your part at all.

There's no danger. The deck stewards won't let anyone swim if it isn't safe.

Dancing in a storm is also great fun. One minute you feel as if you're climbing a steep hill, the next you're skittering down again. The orchestra plays gamely on, and everyone daring

Slosh! Slosh! The rolling sea creates waves in the pool.

enough to be out on the floor has a terrific time.

When the storm dies down, or even on a bright day when there's a lot of mist in the air, look for rainbows. You don't see them often, but watch for them when there is mist over the wake and the sun is astern. Rainbows like to dance in sea spray just off a ship's stern.

Here is another experience unique to ship travel. On a clear day you can prove to yourself that the world is round. On land, when you look at the horizon you see a straight line. But high up on a ship at sea you can see the earth's curve. If you revolve slowly, you will see the horizon going around you in a perfect circle.

I'll end this chapter with stowaways. It used to be easier to stow away on the QE2 than it is now. The QE2 and other Cunard ships have stopped allowing bon voyage parties, those big bashes where hundreds of visitors come aboard just before sailing time. Many ships still have them, however.

Not all the visitors got off. Sometimes, for a lark or just through carelessness, a visitor would be left aboard. If he fessed up right away and bought a ticket, he would be treated like a regular passenger. But anyone who tried to get away with stowing away would probably be caught.

On the QE2 stowaways are locked in a small cabin, fed — nothing fancy — and arrested upon landing. The QE2 still has as occasional stowaway. Perhaps someone manages to sneak aboard the crew gangway, though it isn't easy to do.

When the ship's security people find out there is a stowaway, they start looking for him. . . . Wait! I hear you say. If he's stowed away and they haven't caught him yet, how do they know he's there?

Several ways. A crew member may see someone shaving in one of the public room bathrooms. (Stowaways are usually men.) Of course, the stowaway has no cabin to shave and wash in, or keep luggage in. The bedroom stewards know everyone in the cabins. If you don't have a cabin, you can't eat in the dining room because the restaurant managers have lists of everyone by cabin number.

Stowaways will be observed eating a lot at tea, and at eleven o'clock bouillon, and from the buffet. Also, they wear the same clothes all the time. Once the security people know a stowaway is aboard, it's not too hard to catch him. Then come the locked cabin, the boring food, and the arrest.

There once was a stowaway on the *QE2* who was locked up for the whole voyage but never arrested.

His name was Piccolo, and he was a stray dog who, as far as I know, still lives near the Cunard pier in New York City. Piccolo stowed away when the *QE2* was going on a Bahamas cruise. He was put in the kennels, where he had the whole place to himself, plenty to eat, and the full-time company of the kennel maids.

When the ship returned to New York, she was met by newspaper reporters and television crews, there to do stories on the stowaway dog. Piccolo was a celebrity.

7

Abandon Ship

"Sinking fast . . ."

ONE OF THE FINAL TRANSMISSIONS FROM THE *Titanic*,
April 1912

The most famous of all ocean liners never completed a single voyage. On Wednesday, April 10, 1912, the White Star liner *Titanic* sailed from Southampton on her maiden voyage. Her owners confidently promoted her as unsinkable. Shortly before midnight on Sunday, she hit an iceberg and sank, taking over fifteen hundred passengers and crew with her to the bottom of the Atlantic.

In just ten seconds, the iceberg made a three-hundred-foot gash in the ship's side. Three hours later, tipped almost vertical in the water, the *Titanic* plunged headfirst to the seabed two-and-a-half miles below.

There she remained, 850 miles northeast of the Massachusetts coast, 13,000 feet straight down, undisturbed for seventy-three years.

In 1985 an expedition from Woods Hole Oceanographic Institution in Massachusetts, led by marine geologist Dr. Robert

D. Ballard, located the wreck and took photographs that were published around the world. Ten months later the expedition returned to the site to study the wreckage further.

Dr. Ballard's historic second expedition sailed from Woods Hole in July 1986 aboard the research vessel *Atlantis II*. The ship carried a three-person submersible vehicle called *Alvin*. On July 14 the *Alvin* landed on the bow and bridge of the *Titanic*. With Dr. Ballard in *Alvin* were the pilot — Ralph M. Hollis — and Martin Bowen. In the days that followed, *Alvin* sent the robot video camera Jason Jr. — nicknamed the "floating eyeball" — into the ship's interior. There it took thousands of fascinating pictures of the sunken liner.

It's almost impossible to imagine what Dr. Ballard and his colleagues must have felt when *Alvin* first touched down on the deck of the *Titanic*. In various statements about the expedition, Dr. Ballard spoke of the "eerie feeling" given them by

1912 — The "unsinkable" *Titanic*, shortly before her maiden voyage.

looking at the first photos of the ship's interior. "It was a breathtaking experience," he was quoted in *Time*, and he described the sensation of first landing on the *Titanic* as "like landing on the moon."

One of the expedition's most significant discoveries, or rather lack of discoveries, may change how history tries to explain the *Titanic* tragedy. Dr. Ballard found no trace of the three-hundred-foot gash that for seventy-four years was believed to have caused the ship to sink. He did find evidence that the collision with the berg may have caused enough other damage to destroy the ship. Nothing is conclusive. The gash may well be buried in the seabed, never to be seen again. Some experts believe in the three-hundred-foot gash. Others think a differ-

1986 — On the bottom of the North Atlantic, a robot camera took this picture of *Titanic* bollards, used to secure mooring lines.

ent kind of hull damage caused the liner to sink. We may never know.

From the day the first Ballard expedition located the *Titanic* wreck, there has been talk of raising the ship. Dr. Ballard believes the wreck is too fragile and will never be raised.

Greedy scavengers have also talked of plundering the wreck for the valuables belonging to the many millionaire passengers aboard, and also for anything to sell as souvenirs. They'll have to find her first. Dr. Ballard is not releasing her exact location. The cost of a scavenging expedition may also be prohibitive. The Woods Hole expedition was largely funded by the U.S. Navy in exchange for testing the navy's video robot.

Because of the condition of the wreck and its location, Dr. Ballard believes treasure hunters won't be able to profit from the *Titanic* tragedy. "The *Titanic* will protect itself," he said. I hope he's right.

The *Titanic* never loses her fascination. Numerous books have been written about the tragedy. The best is Walter Lord's *A Night to Remember*. In 1986 Mr. Lord wrote an updated book about the sinking.

Nineteen eighty-seven is a big *Titanic* year, the seventy-fifth anniversary of the tragedy. Each year, the *Titanic* Historical Society remembers the fifteen hundred souls lost on the ship by dropping a wreath in the area where she went down.

Other great twentieth-century ocean liners have met terrible ends, often during wartime. On May 7, 1915, early in World War I, the Cunard liner *Lusitania* was torpedoed off the coast of Ireland by a German submarine and 1,198 people died, many of them Americans.

The first great express liners, *Mauretania* and *Aquitania*, were turned into troopships by the British government during World War I. They survived the war, but so many ships were lost that steamship companies spent much of the 1920s rebuilding their passenger fleets.

During the World War II years (1939–45), passenger ships again were used as troop carriers and also as hospital ships. The first *Queen Elizabeth* and the *Queen Mary* carried 1.5 million soldiers during those years. On a day in 1943, the *Mary* carried 16,683 people from New York to Scotland. Britain's Prime Minister Winston Churchill credited the *Queen*s with shortening the war by at least a year.

The French liner *Normandie*, one of the most beautiful ships ever built, became a war victim in a particularly tragic way. Early in the war, the *Normandie* arrived in New York City.

Aboard the *Queen Mary* during World War II, troops always wore life jackets on deck.

Still smoldering from the senseless fire that destroyed her, the once lovely *Normandie* lies at her New York pier in early 1942.

France had fallen to Hitler's Germany, and the ship could not go safely home again. After the United States entered the war on December 7, 1941, the U.S. government took over the *Normandie*, intending to turn her into a troopship.

Several weeks later, through the carelessness of a workman, the *Normandie* caught fire. The water used to fight the fire caused a shift in the ship's balance. At 2:45 A.M. on February 10, 1942, the beautiful *Normandie*, destroyed by fire, water, and stupidity, rolled over onto her port side. She lay there for eighteen months. At last, in the summer of 1943, salvage operations began. It was mid-September before the liner floated again.

Having gone to all that trouble, the navy no longer wanted

to put any more effort and expense into the *Normandie.* She was anchored for three years, before being sold for scrap, in the Erie Basin off the coast of Brooklyn and close to New York City. The Erie Basin was the winter storage area for Erie Canal boats. The piers are crumbling now, the cargo sheds derelict. I've been there, and it is one eerie basin, no matter how you spell it. I can easily believe that the ghost of the *Normandie* haunts it still.

The first *Queen Elizabeth*, like the *Normandie,* died by fire. At least the magnificent *Elizabeth,* launched in 1940, served nobly during World War II and brought pleasure to 3,200,000 passengers during twenty-eight years as an ocean liner.

In 1968, when Cunard decided to retire her, the *Queen Elizabeth* was sold to a group of U.S. businessmen who wanted to make a Florida tourist attraction out of her. When that venture failed, she was sold to C. Y. Tung of Orient Overseas Line. He had her renamed *Seawise University* and sent to Hong Kong to be converted into a floating university. On January 9, 1972, with the conversion almost finished, the ship caught fire and burned for three days. Completely burned out, almost certainly by arson, she lay on her side, a rusting hulk, until being scrapped years later.

In a bizarre postscript to the *Elizabeth*'s story, a movie company used her as a huge grotesque prop in the James Bond film *The Man with the Golden Gun.*

Like the old *Queens* and so many other ocean liners, the *QE2* has also gone to war. In the spring of 1982, Britain suddenly became involved in a war with Argentina. That country's military government had invaded the tiny Falkland Islands in the South Atlantic off the coast of Argentina.

The Falklands are a British crown colony whose eighteen hundred residents, almost all of them British citizens, make their living by raising sheep and exporting wool. Several thousand Argentine troops were sent to overpower the eighty-four British marines stationed in the islands.

The United Nations demanded that the Argentine forces leave the Falklands. The Argentine government refused to get out. Fighting started on May 1. The British sank an Argentine cruiser. The Argentines sank the British destroyer *Sheffield*. Later, Argentina sank the British warships *Ardent, Coventry,* and *Antelope.* By May 4, when the *QE2* returned from a transatlantic crossing, she had been requisitioned by the British government for service to transport troops and supplies to the Falklands campaign. Then she would return the wounded to England. Turning her into a warship began the next day, and in a week she was ready.

A helicopter pad was put in place on the forward deck area, and a double pad placed astern over the Quarterdeck and One Deck swimming pools. Pictures, plants, much of the furniture, casino equipment, china, glass, and silver were taken ashore to be stored. Sheets of hardboard were put over all the carpets.

One thousand *QE2* crew members volunteered to make the dangerous voyage into the war zone. Six hundred fifty, including thirty women, were chosen to go with the ship. Another woman on board was Linda Kitson, an artist commissioned by the Imperial War Museum to make drawings of the task force.

At dawn on May 12, with regimental bands to pipe them aboard, the three thousand men of the Fifth Infantry Brigade began boarding the ship. The *QE2* sailed for the South Atlantic on May 13, past thousands of family and friends come to wish her well.

Speed was the *QE2*'s main defense against air attack. Her goal was South Georgia Island, eight hundred miles from the

In the South Atlantic, helicopters practice landing on pads covering the *QE2*'s aft swimming pools.

Falklands. She needed to get there as fast as possible, unload her troops and supplies, and return before the enemy could locate her and send bombers after the huge target the *QE2* represented.

Nearing the danger zone, the ship traveled in blackout conditions. How do you black out the scores of portholes and huge windows on a thousand-foot ocean liner? With the same black plastic that garbage bags are made of. The job took three days, and when the ship's helicopters flew around her at night, they reported that she was practically invisible from a mile away.

Fog added to the danger. Icebergs were sighted, and soon the ship was surrounded by them. At one point the ship's radar indicated over one hundred bergs in the area, the largest of them over a mile long. The ship passed through the ice field at night. Next morning, a rising sun reflecting on the last of the bergs made rainbows of orange, red, and yellow.

The *QE2* reached South Georgia on May 27 and anchored in

Cumberland Bay East, a mile from shore. She was not alone. A liner named *Canberra* had arrived from England the day before, along with several other vessels that would transport troops from the *QE2* to the fighting. It was not considered advisable to take the *QE2* closer to the Falklands. But the *Canberra* was in the thick of the fighting. After transporting her troops, she served as a hospital ship.

On May 29 the *QE2* became the world's largest hospital ship as 640 survivors of the sunken naval vessels *Ardent, Antelope,* and *Coventry* were brought aboard. Soon afterward the *QE2* sailed for home. Argentina gave up on June 14, and three days later the country's president resigned.

The *QE2* returned home to Southampton on June 11, after having steamed 14,967 miles. Her homecoming was an emotional one. The lost warships' survivors lined the decks along with the *QE2*'s crew. As they approached their home port, the royal yacht *Britannia* came out to greet them. On board was Queen Elizabeth II's mother, affectionately called the Queen Mum. She sent a radiogram to the *QE2*'s captain, Peter Jackson. A copy of it, and other Falklands War articles, are displayed on the *QE2*.

QE2 escaped harm on her trip to the South Atlantic. But during the past thirty years, luxury liners have had other enemies. With the jet plane providing cheap transportation and fuel and labor costs rising drastically, many ocean liners were taken out of service and sold for scrap or otherwise disposed of.

An explosive end awaited the *Ile de France*. The French Line operated many handsome ships — the *Liberté,* the *Flandre,* and the *France* among them — but one of the most popular and successful on the North Atlantic was the elegant *Ile de France*.

In service since 1927, except for the war years when she served as a troopship, the *Ile de France* reached the end of her useful life in 1959. The French Line sold her for scrap to a Japanese company. Renamed *Furanzu Maru* — "French ship" in Japanese — she sailed for a scrapyard in Japan. But first the scrapyard owners rented the *Ile de France* to Metro-Goldwyn-Mayer for four thousand dollars a day so that the Hollywood movie studio could blow her up for a film called *The Last Voyage,* starring Robert Stack and Dorothy Malone. The script called for a passenger liner to have a boiler explode in the mid-Pacific. The producer was looking for dramatic realism — a real boiler exploding, real bulkheads collapsing, a real funnel falling in.

Obligingly, MGM agreed to blow up the ship in coastal waters so the Japanese salvage operation could be carried out easily. And that is how the *Ile de France* died, blown to bits for a Hollywood movie.

The Last Voyage is still shown on television. If you see it, remember that those explosive scenes weren't filmed with models in a back-lot tank. That macabre prop was once the beautiful *Ile de France.*

The 1960s and 1970s were the darkest time for ocean liners. Many were scrapped or destroyed in other ways. A few ships found happier moorings. The *Queen Mary* became a hotel ship and convention center in Long Beach, California.

Old ships aren't abandoned now the way they were only twenty years ago. With ship travel more popular than it ever was, ships that might have been scrapped are finding a whole new life. More than two dozen new cruise ships have been built in the last few years and more — big and small — are being planned.

We're living in a good time for passenger ships. All kinds of adventures await ship travelers. Some adventures weren't on the original schedule.

8

Every Broken Pump Has a Silver Lining

QE2's Failure Delights Port

<small>HEADLINE IN FALMOUTH, ENGLAND, NEWSPAPER</small>

"This is the captain speaking. It is with deep regret that I have to tell you that the *QE2* has developed engine problems which may prevent temporarily the completion of our voyage to New York. We have turned back toward the entrance to the English Channel, where we will be in touch with the shore as we evaluate various possibilities. I will keep you informed."

And keep us informed he did, frequently, during the next four days. We had sailed from Southampton in early September 1982, a few weeks after the *QE2* had returned to service following her dramatic dash to the South Atlantic with troops for the Falklands campaign.

It had taken only a week to get the ship ready for war. Two-and-a-half months were spent turning her back into a passenger ship. Now she had broken down, and we all wondered what would happen to the crossing we had been looking forward to.

Limping ever more slowly through the Channel, the ship finally anchored just outside Falmouth harbor on the coast of Cornwall, England's westernmost county.

The Falmouth pilot came aboard early Monday afternoon. The pilot boat was followed by the first of countless sightseers. They came out to us in ferryboats and fishing boats, sailboats, rowboats, even kayaks. They sailed around us and waved. We hung over the railings and waved back. Many of our visitors made jokes or offered to give us a tow.

From Monday afternoon until Friday morning when we finally sailed, there was always something going on. One or two local papers were delivered to the cabins each morning. It was fun reading about ourselves and seeing photographs of the ship taken from the shore.

"*QE2*'s Failure Delights Port" was one headline. "Broken Pump Halts *QE2*" was another. A picture caption read "The *QE2* lying off Falmouth — a welcome visitor for local traders who are enjoying a miniboom."

We *QE2* passengers caused Cornwall's miniboom. Ship's tenders were available throughout the day to take people ashore and bring them back to the ship. Tenders are launches carried on a ship to take passengers ashore at ports too small to accommodate a large liner. A tender "tends" to the passengers wanting to visit a port.

The tender ride took about twenty-five minutes. The first thing I saw when I climbed onto the Falmouth dock was a sign offering trips around the *QE2* for two pounds. (The British pound was worth about two dollars that year.) All the local sightseeing boats and ferries and just about any craft that could take passengers charged for the fun of sailing around the *QE2*.

While the residents and tourists in Cornwall were sailing out to look us over, we passengers were sailing into town to look at Cornwall. There were about fourteen hundred passengers on the *QE2*, and most of us abandoned ship by the tenderful to make the most of our unexpected adventure.

The *QE2*'s passengers rented cars and took day trips through the beautiful Cornish countryside. We visited the shops and restaurants and bought everything in sight. Many times people came up to me and asked, "Are you off the *Queen?*" When I said I was, they wanted to hear all about it.

As the days went on, the adventure ended for many passengers. Some people had to get home. More left each day,

First sign of a tourist boom in Cornwall.

most of them sadly. On Thursday several hundred people were flown from a nearby airport to New York on a jumbo jet chartered by Cunard. They got home the day before the ship had been due to arrive.

The rest of us stayed on, thoroughly enjoying ourselves. We went to town, we waved at all the visitors, we listened for reports about the progress of repairs.

While we were still waiting for repairs, we attended a special captain's cocktail party. That gave everyone a chance to look for Falklands ribbons. Each crew member who went on the *QE2* to the South Atlantic earned a medal and a ribbon that is worn on dress clothes. The Falklands ribbon is blue and white, about one-and-a-half inches wide by one-half inch high.

It's easy to spot a Falklands ribbon on a white dress uniform jacket. When you see one, ask the officer about his Falklands experiences. Many of them have fascinating stories. You may also see Falklands ribbons on the dress jackets of waiters and room stewards. You won't see them on seamen or anyone else dressed informally.

It's easy to forget the courage it took for the *QE2* crew members to volunteer for the Falklands campaign. Most of them had no experience of war. Their country needed the *QE2*, and they chose to see the crisis through on the ship. Whenever I see that little blue-and-white ribbon, I think of the darkened *QE2* sailing through a night sea filled with icebergs. I think of her racing back to England with 640 wounded men on board while bombers searched the Atlantic for them.

Finally, four days late and five hundred passengers fewer, we sailed for New York. I watched crew members catch one last fish off the stern. I waved to my last sightseeing boat. Instead of the usual five days, those of us who stayed with the ship had a nine-day adventure.

Shipboard adventures come in all shapes and sizes. Most don't depend on your vessel's engines breaking down. If the usual shipboard activities don't appeal to you or your family, perhaps you should take a theme cruise instead. One of the newest wrinkles in liner travel, theme cruises offer something for every field of interest.

Are you a mystery fan? Several ships have mystery cruises during which a murder is staged and the investigation is carried out by actors who pretend to be regular passengers.

On one mystery cruise the "murder" involved throwing a dummy body overboard. Several people who hadn't realized they were on a mystery cruise got upset. They took to crying "Man overboard!" and frantically calling the Bureau. The next "murder" on that ship will be done a little differently.

If you like sports, there are cruises for both participants and fans. Trips feature tennis and golf pros. Professional athletes go on cruises in the off season, usually with their families. Theme cruises have featured star players from football, baseball, basketball, and hockey teams, as well as Olympic medalists and stars in other sports. The Cunard *Countess* had a fall cruise in 1986 starring members of the World Champion New York Mets baseball team.

Music cruises have been popular for years on several different ships. Classical musicians perform and meet the passengers. In recent years music cruises have branched out into trips featuring jazz, big bands, rock, and disco.

There are total fitness cruises, foreign language immersion cruises, Mother's Day cruises, cruises taking you to Mark Twain country, on a Christmas shopping spree, or to see fall foliage either in New England or in the upper reaches of the Mississippi. One ship had an Errol Flynn Nostalgia Week cruise. Halley's Comet was very big in 1986, and cruises have also been geared to eclipses, jogging, and movies.

On some cruises you can even bring your dog, cat, gerbil, bird, or any pet of moderate size. American Cruise Lines' newest ship — the *New Orleans* — allows passengers to have a pet on board as long as it weighs less than thirty-five pounds and stays in the cabin.

These days it can truly be said that ship travel is for the whole family.

Day Five

"Are we there yet?"

QUESTION NEVER ASKED BY A CHILD ON AN OCEAN LINER

"This is the officer of the watch. Our position at noon today was nine hundred miles due west of Saint Paul's Cathedral."

You're right. That isn't the usual noon announcement of the *QE2*'s position, which involves longitude, latitude, temperature of the air and sea, and other nautical details.

The announcement was made on July 29, 1981, the last full day of a crossing from New York. Most of us aboard had spent the morning listening to radio coverage of the royal wedding of Prince Charles and Lady Diana, which took place in London's Saint Paul's Cathedral. There was no television satellite hookup available for special occasions then.

The *QE2* celebrated the wedding all day long. A map of London showing the route of the royal procession to the Cathedral appeared on the cover of the daily program, together with a copy of the telegram sent from the ship:

THEIR ROYAL HIGHNESSES THE PRINCE AND PRINCESS OF
WALES, BUCKINGHAM PALACE:
The Ship's Company and passengers on board RMS *Queen
Elizabeth 2* send their greetings and wish you
many years of happiness together in the future.
Arnott Master

The signature refers to Robert Arnott, captain on that crossing.

All the public rooms were decorated with the British colors —
red, white, and blue — and posters of the royal couple. There
was champagne on the house, or rather the ship, and a special
menu at dinner.

Each passenger received a medallion struck for the occasion.
About the size of a silver dollar, it had the newlyweds in
profile on one side and the QE2 on the other.

Royal weddings don't come along every day, but it's a rare
voyage that doesn't have diversions not listed in the program.
Many steamship lines make a point of noting birthdays when
they look at passports. Anyone with a birthday during the trip
will have a cake and singing even without calling it to
someone's attention.

When I'm at a table with someone who is having a birthday
or a wedding anniversary, I like to buy a card and get it filled
with signatures. If you try this, approach people you know
around the ship — crew members, Ping-Pong opponents, the
person at the next computer or sunning by the pool. You will
find there are two kinds of people in the world. One kind of
person says, "Hey, great idea, where do I sign?" The other
kind says, "But I don't know them." They'll sign, too, in the
end. I've never been turned down yet.

Fifth day on the QE2 is the day for what on an English ship
is called the children's fancy dress — a costume party. The

adults often have one, too, but the children's fancy dress gets more competitors.

Your younger sister has spent much of her time up in the playroom on Sports Deck. The attendants help the children with their costumes. Or you might want to do a double act, in which case you'll want to bring your sister to the teen club, where the teen counselors have materials and ideas for costumes.

Your sister would be perfect for my favorite costume of all time. I saw it on a little girl the first time I was on the *QE2*, during the ship's first year, 1969. There were over two hundred children under the age of twelve on that crossing, and almost half of them entered the fancy dress. My favorite was dressed in a sheath of bright-green crêpe paper that covered her from head to foot and had an opening down the front. In

Fancy dress aboard the *Stella Solaris*.

the opening, from chin to toes, was a row of green balloons. She was, of course, a pea pod.

A few people bring costumes on board. But it's much more fun to be inventive and, with the help of the counselors, make up a costume from the teen club supplies. People come dressed as buildings, celebrities, animals, the captain. Not long ago I saw three young brothers come as an oil slick.

By the fifth day of a crossing, you may have tried many sports and joined in games such as Trivial Pursuit. You may have been sorely tested by the hard questions in the daily quiz, made up by the librarians. If you'd like to turn the tables and ask hard questions of your own, I have two to get you started.

Ask people around the ship how many propellers there are. Not every crew member will get it right. I'm giving you the number for the *QE2*; you'll have to do your own checking on any other ship, but the principle remains the same.

A person who fancies he knows about ships will say two. People who don't know about ships at all will look at you and say, "Propellers?"

Two is the wrong answer. The ship buff who thinks he or she is pretty smart will say four because a ship fan knows that the *QE2*, in addition to two propellers on the stern, has two more called "bow thrusters" that are used to help the ship maneuver in tight spots. But four isn't the answer either.

The answer is thirty-two. People always forget to count the props on the lifeboats, you see. A nifty question. I'd go up to Boat Deck and count, though, before asking it. A few years ago, *QE2* acquired two big launches for taking passengers ashore during cruises. These boats have two props each. More could be added, so it's safer to count. Ask the question in the teen club. Pretty soon Boat Deck will be full of people counting propellers.

Here's another tricky question. It has absolutely nothing to do with ships, but I learned it on a ship and I love it. It separates children from adults. Adults hardly ever get the answer right, children almost always do.

Study the drawing and decide where X, Y, and Z go — above or below the line. They don't all have to go in the same place. The answer is at the end of the chapter.

```
A      EF  HI  KLMN              T  VW
──────────────────────────────────────
   BCD    G    J         OPQRS   U
```

Quick! Where do the letters X, Y, and Z go?

Other questions asked on ships always include, "Is this your first voyage?" When you answer yes, don't be depressed if it turns out the questioner has been on ships for years.

Ship travelers always seem to be competing for the largest number of crossings on the most famous ships. To have been on the maiden voyage of a famous ship is the greatest coup of all. The *QE2*'s maiden voyage was in 1969, but her story starts years before.

There are two main stages in the building of an ocean liner, once the planning has been done. On July 4, 1965, exactly 125 years after the maiden voyage of Cunard's first ship, the *Britannia*, the keel was laid for the *QE2*.

That first piece of the ship was a 180-ton section of steel. It was put into position in the same berth at what is now called Upper Clyde Shipbuilders in Scotland from which the old *Queens*, the *Elizabeth* and the *Mary*, had been launched. Incidentally, the *Mayflower* is thought to have weighed 180 tons, the same weight as just the first piece of the *QE2*.

For the next twenty-six months, as many as twenty-five hundred people worked on the ship — fitting the machinery,

Queen Elizabeth II inspects the newest Cunard liner before launching her.

doing all the structural work. Until September 1967 the ship lay landlocked in her berth.

Then on September 20 came the launching. Elizabeth II, queen of England, stood on a platform high up near the ship's bow, and christened the ship with the words, "I name this ship *Queen Elizabeth the Second*. May God bless her and all who sail in her." Then the queen cried, "Oh, look at her. She's beautiful!" Elizabeth cut a ribbon sending a bottle of champagne crashing onto the bow in a traditional ceremony. The queen used the same scissors that her mother had used to launch the first *Queen Elizabeth* and that her grandmother had used to launch the *Queen Mary*. As the champagne foamed, the great ship slid out of the berth and floated for the first time.

It took nearly two more years to get the liner ready to sail. The launching is a major test of the engines and general seaworthiness of a ship. Once she is in the water, the liner is fitted out. The bridge, mast, and funnel are put in place, the lifeboats set, and the fourteen hundred public rooms and cabins decorated.

Finally, on May 2, 1969, the work was completed and the *QE2* sailed out of Southampton on her maiden voyage, to the cheers of thousands who came to see her off. When she arrived in New York harbor, she was met by a flotilla of vessels as she neared the Verrazano Narrows Bridge, which guards the entrance to the harbor.

Passing through the Upper Bay, with the Statue of Liberty to port and the Manhattan skyline straight ahead, the *QE2* was surrounded by boats of every size. Fireboats from the New York Fire Department shot towering streams of water into the air.

The mayor, the press, and all sorts of famous people came out to meet the *QE2*. Hundreds of boats in the harbor tooted their horns in welcome, and the *QE2*'s whistle answered them. It was one of the most spectacular welcomes anyone could remember.

An earlier maiden voyage, the *Normandie*'s, was also spectacular. Ocean liner buffs are an opinionated lot. They will argue endlessly about which was the best ship ever to sail.

There are still people around who remember the first *Mauretania* as the greatest ship. Some plump for French ships — the *Liberté* or the *Ile de France* — and some for Italian liners — the *Raffaello* or the *Michelangelo*. The *France*, now the

Norway, was adored by many people, and the old *Queen*s also have devoted fans. I've talked to people who admired certain ships, or were in awe of them, or recalled perfect crossings on this ship or that. No ship seems to have been as genuinely loved as the *Queen Mary*. Even today, people who sailed on her get a little teary remembering their trips. "There was nothing like the old *Mary*," they say.

The *Normandie* was the most modern, sleek, and glamorous of liners, and many consider her the most beautiful ship ever built. Her maiden voyage to New York (she arrived on June 3, 1935) was one big party and produced a fascinating footnote to the history of both ocean liners and baseball.

The *Normandie* sails up the Hudson River on her maiden voyage in 1935.

The *Normandie* can take credit for ending the career of Babe Ruth, possibly the greatest baseball player in history. I first heard this intriguing story during a New York Mets broadcast. It was told by Ralph Kiner, Hall of Fame home-run hitter, charmer, and master of the play-by-play.

Near the end of his career, the stout, party-loving, forty-year-old Ruth was playing for the Boston Braves, after being released by the Yankees, with whom he had his glory years. The aging star still had some pop in him, as baseball people say. He popped three home runs on May 25, 1935.

A few days later, friends in New York invited him to a party to celebrate the arrival of the *Normandie*.

Ruth asked the team's owner for a few days off. When the owner refused, Babe Ruth quit baseball on the spot.

Quiz answer: The letters X, Y, and Z belong above the line. All the letters above the line are made up of straight lines; all the letters below the line are made up of curved lines.

In Southampton, England, this moving monument to the *Titanic's* engineers, all of whom died, was paid for by engineers around the world.

10

Arrival–Don't Forget to Write

This precious stone set in a silver sea . . .
This blessed plot, this earth, this realm, this
England.

SHAKESPEARE, *Richard II*

Although the *QE2* won't get to Southampton until late after-noon, the last day aboard is a muddled kind of time. There are mixed emotions, last-minute activities, and conversations with new friends soon to disappear, often forever.

Shipboard friendships is a term used to describe friendships that begin quickly in the artificial atmosphere of a ship and end as you walk down the gangway. Don't believe everything you hear. Some of my best friends are ship friends.

At your last dinner aboard, or on the last morning, do as the old hands do — get addresses. You may never use them, or you may send one postcard and forget the whole thing. But you never know. One of the English friends you've made on the voyage may invite you for a visit while you're in Europe. There will probably be Americans who live near you back home or with whom you'd like to keep in touch. Ship friendships come on fast and can end just as fast. Or they can last, given the chance.

I talked to twelve-year-old Giles Pugatch about making friends on board ship. Giles is from Montclair, New Jersey, and he had been on the *QE2* before I met him. He had also been on a Bahamas cruise aboard the *Scandinavia*. He'd already made ten or eleven friends and said he always gets addresses from people he meets on ships. He thinks it's easy to make friends on a ship.

One way to make the prospect of leaving the ship less awful is to start thinking of other voyages. The *QE2* Bureau has brochures on future sailings of all the Cunard-owned ships. Although the *QE2* is the only ship making regular transatlantic crossings, several other ships make what are called "positioning cruises." Ships that in the spring and summer have been doing European cruises spend the winter in the Caribbean. When they change position in spring and fall, they do a transatlantic crossing.

Another ship making several crossings a year is the little *Stefan Batory* out of Montreal. A Polish ship, she calls at English and Dutch ports on the way to Gdynia in Poland.

You will find two special sections at the end of this book for ship-related activities you might enjoy between crossings or cruises.

Time is oddly distorted on a ship. One minute you may feel you've been away from home for weeks. The next it will seem as if the time has flown away on the sea winds.

In a real sense, the last day of your *QE2* crossing is two hours shorter. Because the time in England is five hours ahead of that in New York, you have to make up the time somehow. On the *QE2* the first and last nights are normal length. On each of the three middle nights, clocks are advanced an hour.

Then during the last, unsettled day, the clocks go ahead two hours during lunch.

Now is the time to say good-bye, or maybe just "See you again" to your shipboard friends. You rush about buying last-minute souvenirs and a few more photos. Tips are given out to the staff. Tipping is a big worry to many people, but it shouldn't be. Ask the Bureau or the dining-room managers. They will suggest a fair, reasonable amount, and explain the procedure.

Your first transatlantic crossing is almost over. Earlier this last morning, the QE2 left the Atlantic Ocean and entered the English Channel. For several hours she has been moving through the Channel, that stretch of water that lies between England and France.

About noon, the ship made a gentle left turn and sailed past a large island called the Isle of Wight. For all of you up on the deck, the ship's loudspeakers described what you were seeing.

You may have heard the ship's whistle toot three times soon after the ship turned out of the Channel. That's the signal captains sometimes use to alert their families living nearby that they are almost home.

On a clear, sunny day, the river leading to Southampton is a wonderful place to sail. Robin Skelcher, who has been around the world on the QE2 a dozen times, says that there is no more beautiful harbor approach on earth.

You hurried through lunch so you could get back on deck again for the final hours. Tugs have come out to meet the ship and nose her gently along. The pilot has come aboard, and his flag flies from the mast.

The QE2 arrives at the pier. She has come home. On shore the hawsers are secured, the gangways moved into position. Crew members with leave are hurrying off the ship and greet-

QE2's Upper Deck after all the passengers have gone ashore. She quietly awaits her next group of ocean voyagers.

ing families on the dock. You and the other passengers will stay on the ship for another hour or two until all the luggage has been unloaded.

In the Queen's Room, an orchestra is playing and champagne is being served, compliments of the line. Your parents are having one last dance, and your sister is saying good-bye to masses of small children.

Now you stand at your favorite spot on the rail, watching the bustle on the dock far below. You may catch a glimpse of crew friends going home for the night before tomorrow's sailing. Eager as you are to begin the next part of your trip, there is a sadness about leaving this exciting ship where you have spent five days that went by like five minutes, or like a little lifetime.

Be of good cheer. Oceans and rivers cover much of the world. Passenger ships sail those millions of miles of waterways year-round. You are an experienced ship traveler now. This is only the beginning.

You've had a good crossing. I wish you many more happy voyages. May all your wakes have rainbows. And may you often again hear those words that promise adventure: Welcome aboard!

A rare picture of the *QE2*'s propellers, seen only in dry dock or just before launching.

The Peabody Museum of Salem

Bibliography

Bathe, B. W. *Seven Centuries of Sea Travel: From the Crusaders to the Cruises.* New York: Leon Amiel, 1973.

Braynard, Frank O., and William H. Miller. *Fifty Famous Liners 2.* New York: Norton, 1985.

Cruising With Children: An Information Guide. New York: Travel With Your Children, 1986.

Dickens, Charles. *American Notes for General Circulation.* Great Britain: Penguin, 1972 (first published, 1842).

Dodman, Frank E. *The Observer's Book of Ships.* London: Warne, 1973.

Johnston, Paul Forsythe. *Steam and the Sea.* Salem, Massachusetts: Peabody Museum of Salem, 1983.

Maxtone-Graham, John. *Liners to the Sun.* New York: Macmillan, 1985.

———. *The Only Way to Cross.* New York: Macmillan, 1972.

Rentell, Philip. *Historic Cunard Liners.* Cornwall, England: Atlantic Transport Publishers, 1986.

Warwick, Ronald, and William Flayhart III. *QE2.* New York: Norton, 1985.

Wright, Carol. *Queen Elizabeth 2 Cookbook.* London: Michael Joseph, 1983.

The *New York Times*, the *New York Post*, the *Wall Street Journal*, *Travel & Leisure*, *Gourmet*, the *Times* of London, the *Daily*

Telegraph of London, numerous brochures and information releases from Cunard Line and other shipping lines.

Additional Reading

Armstrong, Warren. *Atlantic Highway*. New York: John Day, 1962.

Arnott, Captain Robert Harry. *Captain of the Queen*. England: New English Library, 1982.

Brinnin, John Malcolm. *The Sway of the Grand Saloon: A Social History of the North Atlantic*. New York: Delacorte, 1971.

Coleman, Terry. *The Liners*. London: Penguin, 1976.

Cooper-Hewitt Museum. *The Oceanliner: Speed, Style, Symbol*. New York, 1980.

Lord, Walter. *The Night Lives On: New Ideas on the* Titanic *Disaster*. New York: Morrow, 1986.

———. *A Night to Remember*. New York: Holt, Rinehart & Winston, 1955.

Maxtone-Graham, John. *Tribute to a Queen*. Lausanne: Berlitz, 1987.

Shaum, John H., Jr., and William H. Flayhart III. *Majesty at Sea: The Four-Stackers*. New York: Norton, 1981.

Taylor, Arthur. *Great Liners*. Southampton, Hants., England: Southern Newspapers, n.d.

Maritime Museums/Passenger Ship Collections to Visit in the United States

Maine Maritime Museum, 963 Washington Street, Bath, ME 04530

Peabody Museum, East India Square, Salem, MA 01970

Hudson River Maritime Museum, Kingston, NY 12401

American Merchant Marine Museum Foundation at the

United States Merchant Marine Academy, Kings Point, NY 11024-1699

South Street Seaport Museum, 203 Front Street, New York, NY 10038

Philadelphia Maritime Museum, 321 Chestnut Street, Workshop on the Water, Penn's Landing Boat Basin, Philadelphia, PA 19106

Steamship Historical Society Collection at the University of Baltimore Library, 1420 Maryland Avenue, Baltimore, MD 21201

Chesapeake Bay Maritime Museum, Saint Michaels, MD 21663

Mariners Museum, Newport News, VA 23606

Ships of the Sea Museum, 503 River Street, Savannah, GA 31401

Ohio River Museum and the steamer *W. P. Snyder, Jr.*, 601 Front Street, Marietta, OH 45750

Mississippi River Museum at Mud Island, River Center on Mud Island, Memphis, TN 38103

San Diego Maritime Museum, 1306 North Harbor Drive, San Diego, CA 92101

The Queen Mary, Pier J, Port of Long Beach, CA 90801

National Maritime Museum of San Francisco, Golden Gate National Recreation Area, Foot of Polk Street, San Francisco, CA 94109

Columbia River Maritime Museum, Inc., 792 Marine Drive, Astoria, OR 97103

In Canada

Marine Museum of Upper Canada, Exhibition Place, Toronto, Ontario, Canada M6K 3C3

Maritime Museum of British Columbia, Bastion Square, Victoria, British Columbia, Canada V8W 1H9

The Hotel Queen Mary, well worth a visit.

Land Cruising
For Ship Buffs Between Voyages

Visit one of the maritime museums listed in this section. They have both permanent and changing exhibits, and some have ships you can go aboard or even sail in. The *Queen Mary* museum *is* a ship. Many of her public rooms have been restored to the way they were during the more than thirty years that lovely ship was in service. There is a bookstore, and many shops, and exhibits about the *Mary* as a troopship during World War II.

If you are in southern California, try to spend at least one night in the hotel part of the *Mary*. The Hotel Queen Mary uses the first-class cabins and has kept them just as they were. After a night aboard, you begin to get just the faintest notion of why the *Mary* was such a beloved ship.

Go and see a ship off. Cunard, for security reasons, doesn't allow visitors on its ships, but many other lines allow sailing parties. In New York, most weekends except in winter, you will find several ships welcoming visitors aboard. You'll find sailing parties in progress, bands playing, the bars open. Dance, have a soft drink, explore. Then when the "all ashore" is called, go out on the dock to throw streamers and wave the ship away from the shore.

Several Florida ports are home to ocean liners year-round. Miami has the highest passenger traffic of any port in the world. To visit a ship in the port of Miami, there must be one adult in your party who will be asked to leave some identification with the security officer.

In the port of Los Angeles, you may visit a ship if you know a passenger. If you live near a port, look in the phone book under "Port of . . ." or "Port Authority of . . ." and call to ask what the local rules are.

Travel magazines and the travel sections of most newspapers have ads for shipping companies. There is usually a coupon to send in asking for brochures and often a toll-free number you can call. The brochures, full of enticing color photos, make for good reading and even better daydreaming.

You'll find both a wide range of big ships and a trend toward smaller liners going to ports large ships can't reach. For instance, Exploration Cruise Lines has trips from Portland, Oregon, through rivers and lakes to Lewiston, Idaho, the Northwest's most inland seaport. Ships call at more ports around the world than ever before.

It's interesting to look at the pictures of the ships and at the deck plans in those brochures. Every car of the same model and color is a clone of every other. Every 747 is like every other 747. But each ship is unique. If you sail to England on the *QE2*, or to Nassau on the *Norway*, or to Alaska on the *Royal Princess*, or to Hong Kong on the *Golden Odyssey*, or to Minneapolis on the *Delta Queen* you can be sure no other ship will give you the same adventure.

A few years ago it was estimated that one hundred thousand kids made trips on passenger ships. The number increases every year.

Watch a movie that takes place on an ocean liner, or on a movie set made to look like a liner. Such movies often play late at night, but they can be taped for convenient viewing or rented at video stores.

I'd start with two Marx Brothers movies: *Monkey Business* (1931) and *A Night at the Opera* (1935). *Monkey Business* opens with the brothers stowing away in pickle barrels and has lots of chases.

A Night at the Opera has one hilarious scene in which the Marx Brothers give a party in a small cabin that they fill right up to the top with people. You might consider, next time you're on a ship, giving a *Night at the Opera* party with everyone you've met during a crossing. Have it in the smallest cabin you can find.

Here's a selection of other ship movies:

Anything Goes — 1936
Assault on a Queen — 1966
China Seas — 1935
Juggernaut — 1974
The Lady Eve — 1941
The Last Voyage — 1960, the movie using the *Ile de France* for a prop.
Love Affair — 1939
Luxury Liner — 1933
A Night to Remember — 1958, based on Walter Lord's book, it's the best *Titanic* movie. The other one is called *Titanic* (1953).
''Now, Voyager'' — 1942
The Poseidon Adventure — 1972
The Princess Comes Across — 1936
Romance on the High Seas — 1948, the movie that introduced Doris Day.
Ship of Fools — 1965
Stowaway — 1936, starring Shirley Temple and one of her best.

Here's something else to look at, full of ship drawings. Two educational and decorative charts related to ocean liners and suitable for framing, inscribed and autographed by the author, are available as follows: Atlantic Ocean Liners, 21″ × 17″ (from *The Only Way to Cross*), for $7.50, and Cruise Ship Chart, 19½″ × 13″ (from *Liners to the Sun*), for $7.50. Prices include postage and handling. Order both charts for $12.00. Please make check payable to John Maxtone-Graham and mail to 117 West 78th Street, New York, NY 10024.

When you start planning another voyage, you and your family might like to get in touch with TWYCH (the initials stand for Travel With Your Children). This organization publishes a book, updated every year, called *Cruising With Children: An Information Guide.* Its address is 80 Eighth Avenue, New York, NY 10011. The guide gives detailed information on close to one hundred liners and their facilities for young people.

Index

Numbers in *italics* refer to pages with illustrations.